HOUGHTON MIFFLIN HARCOURT

WRITE SOURCE

SkillsBook

GREAT SOURCE®

HOUGHTON MIFFLIN HARCOURT

A Few Words About the *Write Source SkillsBook*

Before you begin . . .

The *SkillsBook* provides you with opportunities to practice the editing and proofreading skills presented in the *Write Source* textbook. The textbook contains guidelines, examples, and models to help you complete your work in the *SkillsBook.*

Each *SkillsBook* activity includes a brief introduction to the topic and refers you to the pages in the textbook that offer additional information and examples. The "Proofreading Activities" focus on punctuation and the mechanics of writing. The "Parts of Speech Activities" highlight each of the eight parts of speech. The "Sentence Activities" provide practice in sentence combining and in correcting common sentence problems.

The Extend

Many activities include an **Extend** at the end of the exercise. Its purpose is to provide ideas for follow-up work that will help you apply what you have learned to your own writing.

Printed in the U.S.A.

ISBN 978-0-547-48467-9

2 3 4 5 6 7 8 0928 15 14 13 12

4500358513 A B C D E F G

CONTENTS

Proofreading Activities

Marking Punctuation

Parts of Speech Activities

Nouns

Pronouns

Verbs

Adjectives & Adverbs

Prepositions, Conjunctions, & Interjections

Sentence Activities

Sentence Basics

Sentence Combining

Sentence Problems

COMMA SPLICES & RUN-ON SENTENCES

SENTENCE FRAGMENTS & RAMBLING SENTENCES

MISPLACED & DANGLING MODIFIERS

WORDINESS & UNPARALLEL CONSTRUCTION

SHIFTS IN CONSTRUCTION

Proofreading Activities

The activities in this section of your *SkillsBook* include sentences that need to be checked for punctuation, mechanics, or correct word choices. Most of the activities also include helpful textbook references. In addition, the **Extend** activities provide follow-up practice of certain skills.

Pretest: Punctuation

Insert missing punctuation (commas, semicolons, colons, apostrophes, hyphens, dashes, parentheses, quotation marks, underlining for italics, and end punctuation) in the following sentences.

1. If youre like most busy active teens youre probably sleep deprived
2. Consider this list of everyday activities watching TV riding in a car reading in an easy chair and sitting while listening to someone talk
3. When was the last time you fell asleep in one of these situations and how often has that happened to you
4. William Dement PhD a highly respected sleep researcher has written The Promise of Sleep a book that explains the importance of a good nights rest
5. According to an article in the Kansas City Star Dement is concerned about the hectic lifestyle most Americans lead we are neglecting our Zs
6. Apathy irritability lack of motivation all of these could be signs that youre not getting enough sleep
7. Dement offers this analysis I believe it is safe to say that the single symptom most frequently found in severe sleep disorders is daytime fatigue
8. Coffee cola tea any beverage containing caffeine may keep you awake therefore you should avoid drinking them in the evening
9. A heavy late evening supper is also a bad idea according to Dement who recommends eating three to four hours before bedtime
10. Erratic sleep patterns confuse your brain so if you want to get the best possible sleep go to bed and get up at about the same time every day

11. A bedtime ritual such as reading a few pages of a book Ive got plenty you can borrow can hasten your trip to dreamland

12. Dement also suggests that a good nights sleep calls for a comfortable bed and a dark quiet well ventilated room

13. Most people need seven to eight hours of sleep a night and teenagers who have growing bodies and devote lots of energy to sports and other physical activities may require even more

14. Have you ever heard of sleep apnea this condition which causes a person to stop breathing numerous times during the night affects about 50 million Americans

15. Dement says that apnea causes 38000 deaths due to heart attacks and strokes each year however that is probably not a large concern at age 17

16. All right Lori wondered aloud but how do I know if I have sleep apnea

17. I doubt you have a sleep disorder Hector replied You probably just need to get to bed earlier

18. Okay Lori said I resolve that starting on January 1 2030 when I am 35 years old I will go to bed every night at 1000 pm and get up at 600 am

End Punctuation

When used in dialogue, a period is always placed inside quotation marks. A question mark or an exclamation point is placed either inside or outside the quotation marks. Turn to 605.4, 606.1, and 632.2 in *Write Source.*

Add end punctuation and capitalize the first word in each sentence below.

"have you ever known a person who was completely unpredictable" I asked my father

"yes," he said, "when I was young, I had a boss who seemed to have two personalities that switched on and off like hot and cold running water it was always one extreme or the other his name was Mr. Bunder—I'll never forget him"

I said to my dad, "do you want to know something I'm having exactly the same experience with my boss, Mr. Selland"

"What's the problem" Dad wanted to know

"Well, it's kind of funny he tries to be a nice guy, and he likes to joke, but when his mood turns sour, things become unbelievably difficult I can't do anything right, and then he complains about some of the silliest and most unimportant things imaginable"

"Wow that's exactly what Mr. Bunder was like," Dad said "sometimes Mr. Bunder complained about other employees, and he would expect me to agree with him even though he knew they were my friends then in another minute he would be kidding again, being overly friendly and clever it was very difficult working with someone so unpredictable I not only had to concentrate on my work, but I also had to be constantly on my guard trying to predict Mr. Bunder's moods"

"That's exactly the way Mr. Selland is they must be related," I said

Review: End Punctuation

Add end punctuation and capitalize the first word in each sentence in the following passage. (*Tip:* Do not delete any commas.)

I was eight the first time I hiked part of the Appalachian Trail back then, I only knew it as a path crossing through a nearby park my friends and I often played along the stretch of trail that ran behind our houses we never walked far, but I always wondered, “Where does this trail come from where does it go”

When I was 16, my father and I spent seven days on the trail, carrying packs almost 50 miles I thought that was long—until Dad reminded me the trail covers more than 2,000 miles from Georgia to Maine, and that 200 to 300 people make the entire trek each year that was all I needed to hear I decided I wanted to be one of them

I started training—walking around my hometown with a full backpack until I could cover five miles an hour without breaking a sweat where could I find good boots and gear I saved money and bought them I learned how to use topographical maps and how to cook outdoors I studied first aid and even learned how to avoid dangerous animals

Two days after my eighteenth birthday, my parents dropped me off at the top of Springer Mountain in Georgia, the southern end of the trail they asked, “Are you ready” was I ever for sixty-six days, I was alone with my thoughts, putting one foot in front of the other when I finally reached the end of the trail at Mount Katahdin, Maine, I was dirty and tired, but I had made it I had followed my dream now I was eager to pursue the next one: a hamburger and a hot bath

Commas with Coordinating Conjunctions

A comma precedes a coordinating conjunction *(and, but, or, nor, yet,* and *so)* when the conjunction joins two independent clauses. Turn to 608.1 in *Write Source*.

Add the missing commas in the following sentences. One sentence is correct.

1. Helen Jackson first wrote about the mistreatment of Native Americans in 1881, but her message did not prevent the Battle of Wounded Knee in 1890.
2. In the third century B.C.E., the Greek astronomer Aristarchus determined that the earth was round but, for the next 14 centuries, most other astronomers still believed it was flat.
3. Janet doesn't have that CD nor does she want it.
4. The day was hot and steamy and the crowd grew restless.
5. Are you going or am I traveling solo?
6. Jim wants to try rock climbing yet I doubt he'd admit it.
7. He looks pretty nervous so we'll have to encourage him.
8. Last year I was caught in a storm and now I always heed the forecast.
9. People on the ground hear sonic booms when a plane travels faster than the speed of sound but the pilot does not hear them.
10. I am going to a movie or I am going skiing.
11. The first deep-sea divers used a breathing device to receive oxygen but the equipment was dangerous.
12. Jacques Cousteau almost drowned twice while using one of these early devices before he figured out the solution: compressed air.
13. To test the first Aqua-Lung, Cousteau and two partners completed 500 dives at depths of 50 to 100 feet and their invention performed perfectly.

Extend: Which sentence does not need a comma? Write a short explanation telling why a comma is unnecessary in that sentence.

Commas in a Series & to Separate Equal Adjectives

Commas separate individual words, phrases, or clauses in a series. A comma is also used to separate two adjectives that equally modify the same noun. Turn to 608.2 and 610.2 in *Write Source*.

Add commas where they are needed in the following sentences.

1. Harry S. Truman Dwight D. Eisenhower and John F. Kennedy were the 33rd 34th and 35th presidents of the United States, respectively.
2. Planets asteroids moons meteors comets—all travel around the sun.
3. Long ago, astronomers believed the sun the moon and the other planets in our solar system circled around the earth.
4. He will need a T-square a compass and a drawing board.
5. A drafting pencil uses long sturdy shafts of lead.
6. That maneuver requires a slow steady hand.
7. He was a very pleasant friendly man.
8. A soft almost imperceptible rustle came from inside the nest.
9. "What a sweet little dog!" she cried.
10. The dull-green parrot had dirty tattered feathers.
11. I love homemade spaghetti sauce with plump ripe tomatoes.
12. I spent the morning reading the newspaper watching the news and surfing the Internet.
13. This afternoon I plan to put together a complete finely-tuned proposal.
14. You will need fresh zucchini tomatoes and basil to make that recipe.
15. Don't plant that creeping quick-spreading mint in your garden.

Extend: In your own words, describe two tests you can use to determine whether adjectives are "equal." Write out your answer and a sentence that uses two equal and two unequal adjectives.

Commas After Introductory Phrases & Clauses

A comma separates an adverb clause (or a long modifying phrase) from the independent clause that follows it. If the independent clause comes first, the comma is usually omitted. See 610.3 in *Write Source.*

Underline the independent clauses in the sentences below and add the missing commas.

1. If you carefully watch the skies above America's mountain ranges and coastal wetlands, you might be lucky enough to spy a bald eagle.
2. Even while soaring lazily on thermal currents the eagle maintains an average speed of roughly 20 mph.
3. Our majestic national bird can reach speeds of up to 100 mph while diving for food.
4. Although it prefers fish to other types of food the bald eagle occasionally eats carrion and waterfowl.
5. While eagles have been known to live up to 40 years in captivity their average life span in the wild is only 20 years.
6. As the bald eagle's worst enemy human beings cause 80 percent of all eagle deaths (through hunting, poaching, and polluting).
7. According to a book I read Benjamin Franklin did not want the bald eagle to be our national bird; he chose the wild turkey instead.
8. Soaring high against the clouds the bald eagle is a magnificent sight even for those who are not true bird-watchers.
9. The bald eagle has been removed from the endangered species list within the last few years.

Extend: Write four sentences about a bird or an animal that interests you. Use independent and dependent clauses.

Review: Commas 1

Add the missing commas in the sentences below. Four sentences are correct as is.

1. We had planned to go cross-country skiing but a blizzard prevented us from even leaving the house.
2. Mr. Johnson has a very round bald head.
3. In place of the tree stump we'll plant a small flower garden.
4. When she finds a better job she'll buy a new car.
5. The colorful tissue box looks out of place in the locker room.
6. By chasing every car that drove past Nori's dog got all the exercise he needed.
7. Sean's favorite foods are shrimp beef stew and any kind of pasta.
8. We can go to the county zoo or hang out at the lakefront.
9. Since we can't do both we must decide which is more appealing.
10. Before you go please wash the breakfast dishes vacuum the stairs and sweep the front porch.
11. The home's dirty weathered siding had not felt a paintbrush in ages.
12. You can ride with me or you can ride with Manuel.
13. Considering the condition of the bike perhaps you'd be better off walking.
14. Tickets for the movie were sold out at the first theater so we drove a few miles farther to the big cinema center on Layton.
15. Grace cut the grass and trimmed the hedges.
16. We didn't pitch our tent that night because they were predicting flash floods.

Commas to Set Off Contrasted Elements & Appositives

Commas set off appositives from the rest of the sentence. Commas may also set off contrasting expressions—phrases or clauses that begin with words such as *not, but, but not, while,* and *though.* Turn to 608.3 and 610.1 in *Write Source.*

Combine each pair of sentences below to create one simple sentence that uses a contrasting expression.

1. Bill won the election. Sally did not win the election.
2. The motel was inexpensive. The motel was no bargain.
3. Juan was born in Puerto Rico. Rubiel was not.
4. Rubiel was born in New York. He is proud of his Hispanic heritage.
5. He is a police officer. He doesn't work in this county.

Set off the appositives in the sentences below with commas.

1. John Riggs and Andrew Vachss two excellent mystery novelists write very different types of mysteries.
2. Garth Ryland the protagonist in Riggs' novels lives in Oakalla a small town in Wisconsin.
3. Ryland the editor of Oakalla's hometown newspaper often finds himself involved in crime-solving through his friendship with Rupert Roberts Oakalla's sheriff.
4. Burke the outlaw antihero of Vachss' books operates in the dark underbelly of New York City.
5. Burke and his "family" a band of social outcasts and misfits constantly antagonize the wrong people in the city.

Extend: Write five sentences describing your favorite fictional detective or another type of character. Use an appositive phrase in each sentence.

Commas with Nonrestrictive Phrases & Clauses 1

Commas set off nonrestrictive clauses and phrases because they are not needed to correctly understand a sentence; they simply add information. Commas do *not* set off restrictive clauses and phrases. See 612.2 in *Write Source.*

Add commas to the nonrestrictive clauses and phrases below. If a sentence contains a restrictive clause or phrase and is correct as is, underline it and write *C* in the blank.

____ **1.** The problem of cutting class, which was almost nonexistent last year, had suddenly mushroomed.

____ **2.** The administration decided that all students who were caught cutting class would face possible suspension.

____ **3.** John's parents who are very strict had frequently warned their son not to cut class.

____ **4.** John who was a senior knew cutting had serious consequences.

____ **5.** But John whose grades were quite good overall didn't think missing a class or two would matter, so he cut English class one day.

____ **6.** The school principal who frequently patrolled the halls between classes noticed John scurrying down a back stairway.

____ **7.** Two teachers who were on break saw John, too.

____ **8.** His English teacher who had given a pop quiz that day decided to give him a zero for the quiz.

____ **9.** John thought that was tough, but the other punishment from his parents losing driving privileges for a month was even tougher.

____ **10.** He had simply failed to heed the warnings he had been given.

____ **11.** The lesson that he learned was an important one.

Extend: Write a paragraph about a time you were punished and lost a privilege. Include at least three sentences containing unnecessary (nonrestrictive) phrases or clauses; remember to place commas correctly.

Commas with Nonrestrictive Phrases & Clauses 2

Clauses and phrases may be restrictive or nonrestrictive. Nonrestrictive clauses and phrases are set off with commas. Turn to 612.2 in *Write Source*.

Underline each restrictive and nonrestrictive clause and phrase and label them *R* for restrictive or *N* for nonrestrictive. Then insert commas where needed.

1. Baseball which has long been considered America's national pastime is receiving stiff competition from football.
2. The Super Bowl which is the high point of the professional football season attracts more than a billion television viewers worldwide.
3. Baseball cannot offer any single game that matches the drawing power of the Super Bowl.
4. College baseball which has almost no television exposure is far less popular than college football.
5. Cable and satellite TV systems now owned by many of us have increased the number of football games we can watch.
6. This increased availability which has increased the number of football fans around the world has helped make football a big-money enterprise.
7. Football its popularity expanding may soon replace baseball as "America's Game."
8. Fans closely following the progress of the NFL each week could argue that football is already number one.
9. Professional football which is now played in Europe may someday replace soccer as "The World's Game."
10. But for now, the sport that attracts the most fans worldwide is still soccer.

Extend: Defend your favorite sport in a paragraph that includes at least three examples of nonrestrictive clauses and phrases. Underline them.

Other Uses for Commas 1

Commas set off interruptions, separate numerals, and enclose titles or initials following a surname. They can also be used for clarity or emphasis. Turn to 616.3, 614.3, 614.4 and 616.5 in *Write Source* for examples.

Insert commas where they are needed in the sentences below.

1. What was said, was said in jest.
2. As a matter of fact Rebecca knew what to expect before she opened the door.
3. The best building materials if you ask me are steel and wood.
4. The jet lifted off the runway and smoothly ascended to its cruising altitude of 35000 feet.
5. Thaddeus J. Smarty Sr. found himself stalled at the intersection in his luxury sedan.
6. Fortunately the engine started again.
7. The best way to learn to swim it is often said is to take lessons.
8. Whatever you do do it with style.
9. More than 100000 people marched in Washington last weekend.
10. Marcus Welby M.D. was a fictitious doctor in an old TV show.
11. Tom I believe is studying medicine at UT.
12. I ran ran as if my life depended on it
13. He had to move much to his mother's dismay.
14. For most people especially older people having health insurance is critical.
15. Because of all the Smiths in my e-mail address book, I had to list them as Smith J. D.; Smith J. R.; and Smith M. W.

Extend: Write five to seven sentences about a subject of your choosing. Illustrate all the uses for commas covered in this exercise: interruptions, numerals, titles, initials, clarity, and emphasis.

Other Uses for Commas 2

View the examples below to see how commas are used to set off nouns of direct address, interjections, and items in addresses and dates. Turn to 616.4, 616.2, 614.2, and 614.1 in *Write Source* for more.

- **Joe, can you give me a ride to the mall?** (The comma sets off the name *Joe,* a noun of direct address.)
- **No way, this couch can't cost that much.** (The comma sets off the interjection *no way.*)
- **My new address will be 72 Brown Street, Apartment 2C, New York, New York 10086.** (The commas set off items in the address.)
- **On July 4, 2005, fire destroyed the warehouse.** (The commas set off the day and year.)

Write sentences using the interjections, nouns of direct address, dates, and street addresses listed below. Add any missing commas.

1. *(yeah)* Yeah, I've been there.
2. *(Dad)* ______
3. *(January 1 2000)* ______
4. *(3600 Howard Avenue Milwaukee Wisconsin 53786)* ______
5. *(oops)* ______
6. *(Spot)* ______
7. *(1600 Pennsylvania Avenue NW Washington D.C. 20006)* ______
8. *(your own birth date)* ______

Review: Commas 2

Insert commas where they are needed in the following sentences.

1. “Sinclair Lewis is, I am sure, one of our 20 greatest American novelists” said Mr. Goldsmith our English teacher.
2. Do you realize class how much such novelists have shaped our thinking?
3. When we read a novel the setting the characters and the story interest us but so do the ideas.
4. Yes whether the ideas in a novel please us or anger us we are nevertheless forced to think about them.
5. Sinclair Lewis known to his family as Harry was born on February 7 1885 in Sauk Centre Minnesota.
6. As a young boy Lewis was homely clumsy and nerdy; consequently he was the object of other children’s cruelty.
7. Lewis was an unhappy friendless child and he found refuge in books.
8. Sinclair Lewis was 28 when he wrote his first novel; but only after his sixth novel *Main Street* was published seven years later did he have real success.
9. *Main Street* which hit the American public like a tornado out of the Midwest was a novel of social criticism.
10. This novel revealed the pettiness of the small town the emptiness of Americans who value material gain as an end in itself and the myth of the small town as a family paradise.
11. On December 10 1930 Sinclair Lewis became the first American writer to win the Nobel Prize for literature.

Semicolons

Semicolons are used in several ways. To check your understanding, turn to 618.1–618.3 in *Write Source*—*after* completing this exercise.

Study the sentences below. Develop a rule that explains how semicolons are used in each set. (This exercise illustrates three different rules.)

Set 1

1. I once had a mountain bike; that was the first bike I ever owned.

2. The venom from the king cobra is the deadliest of all snake poisons; a single gram can kill 150 people.

3. Black holes are areas in which gravity is extremely strong; anything pulled into a black hole cannot get out.

Rule: ____

____

Tip: Study the groups of words before and after the semicolons. What do these groups have in common? Can they stand alone? What other punctuation marks could be used in place of the semicolons?

Set 2

1. A shark has a built-in immunity to nearly every type of bacteria; consequently, it almost never gets sick.

2. The Chicago Cubs are seen across the country on cable television; as a result, they are one of the most popular baseball teams in America.

3. The dinner at the banquet was disappointing; however, the entertainment that followed made up for the lumpy mashed potatoes and rubbery chicken.

Rule: ____

____

Tip: Pay special attention to the words or phrases immediately following the semicolons. What do they have in common? What function do they serve? What additional punctuation mark appears within each sentence? How are these sentences similar to or different from the first set?

Set 3

1. I packed a razor, a toothbrush, and deodorant; blue jeans, a bathing suit, and a jacket; and tennis balls, fishhooks, and golf clubs.

2. For the food drive the store owner provided canned soups, vegetables, and meats; packaged breads, rolls, and crackers; and assorted fruits, nuts, and cheeses.

Rule: ____

____

Tip: Note that each sentence contains several series, or lists of items. How are semicolons used to group the items, and why?

Place semicolons in the following sentences.

1. A charging elephant can move at speeds up to 25 mph ; luckily, most elephant charges are bluffs.

2. Geese are the highest fliers in the bird family some have been known to fly as high as 25,000 feet.

3. A peregrine falcon dives at a speed of 200 mph it leaves everything far behind as it zings along.

4. The white shark is always hungry as a result, it is constantly hunting for food.

5. An ant has the largest brain in proportion to its body the rhinoceros beetle is the strongest animal for its size.

6. Butterflies have taste buds in their feet dogs have sweat pods in theirs.

7. It is true that animals present us with amazing facts—a chameleon will take on the colors of its environment, even if it is blind although a white shark is always hungry, it will rarely attack a person of all living things, the male emperor moth has the keenest sense of smell.

Colons 1

Review the rules for using colons at 620.1–620.6 in *Write Source.*

Insert colons where they are needed below. Some sentences are already correct.

1. Rob has sent for information about universities in these states: Wisconsin, Illinois, California, and Florida.
2. Dear Registrar Please send me your latest catalog. I am interested in . . .
3. One question is very important to anyone seeking a college education How much is it going to cost?
4. Rob made his decision after carefully considering the information about tuition, housing, programs, and financial aid.
5. Here are two other important questions for prospective college students to ask Will I receive a quality education? Will the degree I earn truly prepare me for the career area I have chosen?
6. My father never tires of repeating this bit of advice "These days, you've got to get a good education."
7. As a college freshman, Rob plans to take five courses history, English, geography, chemistry, and math.
8. Freshmen often have to leave their noisy dorms to find two ingredients that are critical to studying peace and quiet.
9. During final exam week, college libraries fill with hardworking students intent on a single goal passing their exams.
10. The freshman year can be exciting, challenging, and fun.

Extend: Identify one colon rule in the textbook that wasn't covered in this exercise and write a sentence that demonstrates its use.

Colons 2

Review the rules for using colons at 620.1–620.6 in *Write Source.*

Add the missing colons in the following sentences. One sentence is already correct.

1. Try this tongue twister: Sally sells seashells by the seashore.
2. Six different words are pronounced *sōl soul, sole, sowl, sol, sowle,* and *soal.*
3. These six words have an unusual distinction they are the largest group of homonyms in the English language.
4. The English word with the most meanings is one we use nearly every day *set.*
5. *Set* has an impressive number of roles 58 noun uses, 126 verbal uses, and 10 uses as a participial adjective.
6. We can thank Adlai Stevenson for this droll statement "Man does not live by words alone, despite the fact that sometimes he has to eat them."
7. Like many words in our language, *tip* is an acronym, derived from the first letters of the words for which it stands *to insure promptness.*
8. The best-selling book of all time is the Bible.
9. One well-known passage is contained in Ecclesiastes 3 1-9; it is a poem about the tragedy of old age.
10. In the 1960s, a rock group called the Byrds turned this Biblical verse into a hit song, adding just three words to the passage *turn, turn, turn.*
11. Only two words in the English language contain all five vowels (*a, e, i, o, u*) in alphabetical order *abstemious* and *facetious.*
12. Many people frequently misspell these words *colonel, precede,* and *thorough.*

Extend: Write five sentences about words, using a colon in a different way in each sentence. See 620.1–620.6 in *Write Source* for examples.

Review: Semicolons & Colons

Insert the missing semicolons and colons in the following sentences. Also add a comma after any conjunctive adverb preceded by a semicolon.

1. Some horse breeds have existed for thousands of years; however, the English thoroughbred has a much shorter history.
2. In the 1700s, some English nobles had a radical idea create a new breed of horse.
3. Large, heavy workhorses were too clumsy the nobles wanted fast, agile horses for hunting, racing, and pleasure riding.
4. Arabian horses were fast however they were also small and hard to obtain.
5. Arabs depended on their horses so much that in some parts of the Middle East horses were legally protected in fact it was a crime to sell your horse.
6. Between 1525 and 1680, three Arabian stallions arrived in England Byerly Turk, Darley Arabian, and Godolphin Arabian.
7. The foals born from these Arabian stallions and English mares were different from their parents they had longer legs and more personality.
8. In 1764, an amazing thoroughbred was born Eclipse.
9. Eclipse was not especially attractive he was clumsy and awkward, and he didn't get along with other horses.
10. But his speed made up for his faults he beat every horse he ever raced.
11. Eclipse was so fast that he inspired a saying "Eclipse first, the rest nowhere."
12. Eclipse is long gone, but he left a permanent mark many thoroughbreds alive today can trace their roots back to him.

Hyphens

Hyphens are used to make compound words (*master-at-arms*), to form new words beginning with prefixes (*ex-governor*), to join numbers showing a life span (1301–1337), and to join two or more words serving as a single adjective (*short-lived*). Turn to pages 624–626 in your *Write Source* textbook for other uses.

Insert hyphens where they are needed in the sentences below.

1. Copernicus lived during the post Middle Ages period (1473 1543).
2. As a 30 year old, he became a graduate of the University of Ferrara.
3. His new ideas were in direct opposition to Ptolemy, a well known second century astronomer.
4. Copernicus first attended the University of Krakow in his native Poland; then he studied liberal arts at Bologna, Italy (1496 1501).
5. When Copernicus was forty one, he wrote a paper that challenged the works of Aristotle.
6. Many of his peers argued against his simpler, sun centered model of the universe.
7. His half radical, half conservative theory used the same physics of motion that Aristotle had used.
8. The Catholic Church, an all powerful group at the time, rejected Copernicus' theories.
9. Twenty six years after he drafted his initial outline, a paper on his new ideas was formally published.
10. Copernicus' fifteenth century breakthroughs have made a huge difference in how we view the universe today.

Extend: Review "Guidelines for Dividing with Hyphens" at 626.5 in *Write Source*. Make a list of any 20 words of more than one syllable from the exercise above. Exchange papers with a classmate. Imagine that each word appears at the end of a line of text and must, if possible, be broken. Mark the correct dividing points with hyphens.

Dashes

Dashes mark interruptions in a sentence, set off introductory lists, and show hesitation in speech. Dashes may also be used to emphasize particular words or phrases, often replacing commas. Turn to page 640 in *Write Source*.

Add dashes where they are needed in the following sentences.

1. Product advertisements whether good, bad, or just plain weird often tell a lot about the society for which they are created. Consider the following vintage advertisements.
2. “Deviled ham, potted ham, beef, and tongue what you need for sandwiches.” (Libby, McNeill & Libby, 1899)
3. “The Sholes Visible Typewriter competes with any machine at any price but at a retail price of $60.00, none can compete with it.” (A. D. Meiselbach Typewriter Company, 1903)
4. “Blow smoke into the bottom of the provision chamber of our refrigerator and you can see the air currents that prove rapid circulation of cold real cold air.” (White Enamel Refrigerator Co., 1906, condensed)
5. “Style, safety, comfort they're all here in the highly efficient Pope-Waverly Electric Stanhouse price, $1,400.” (Pope Motor Car Company, 1906)
6. “Then there's the Timken power-transmitting unit another feature originated by Timken.” (Timken-Detroit Axle Co., 1912)
7. “Humors of the blood, skin, and scalp whether itching, bleeding, crusted, or pimply are speedily, permanently, economically, and infallibly cured by the Cuticura Remedies.” (Potter Drug and Chemical Corporation, 1911, condensed)

Extend: Write a couple of short ads—just two or three sentences long—using dashes in at least two different ways.

Review: Hyphens & Dashes

Insert the missing hyphens and dashes below. (Note that many dashes have been used for the sake of this exercise; as a rule, they should be used more sparingly.)

William Faulkner, F. Scott Fitzgerald, and Ernest Hemingway three of the twentieth century's best known writers all had unique writing styles and lives. As an 18 year old reporter at the *Kansas City Star,* Hemingway following the newspaper's guidelines wrote in short declarative sentences. In contrast, Fitzgerald's after college style was more lyrical and emotional. Faulkner's writing was the most complex of all. He used rambling, stream of consciousness sentences in simple stories. In Faulkner's hands, a single sentence could become a page long monster.

Faulkner (1897 1962) wrote about the South. His brooding novels are filled with intriguing characters troubled ancestors, brutal antiheroes, and shadowy backwoods hermits. Fitzgerald (1896 1940) often wrote about Hollywood about its excesses and the ill fated American dream. Hemingway (1899 1961) penned tales of rugged heroes hunters, soldiers, and bullfighters drawing upon his real life adventures.

Hemingway was the most widely read and also the most widely disliked. He did find a friend in Fitzgerald at least for a time. Later, the two became rivals. After Fitzgerald died, Hemingway dismissed his old friend's writing as "dust on the wings of a butterfly" writing that wouldn't last. In turn, Faulkner criticized Hemingway. About Hemingway's Pulitzer Prize winning novel, *The Old Man and the Sea,* Faulkner once stated, "It's all right. Praise God that whatever made and loves and pities Hemingway . . . kept him from touching it further."

Apostrophes in Contractions & Plurals

An apostrophe shows that one or more letters have been left out of a word, forming a contraction. An apostrophe is also used to form the plural of a letter, a number, a sign, or a word discussed as a word. Turn to 628.1 and 630.4 in *Write Source*.

Insert the missing apostrophes in the following sentences.

1. Don't you ever wonder why clocks run "clockwise"?
2. Its because the first clock makers built the clock's hands to mimic the natural movements of the sun on a sundial.
3. If clocks hadnt been invented in the Northern Hemisphere, anything turning "clockwise" would run in the opposite direction.
4. Would the *1*s, *2*s, and *3*s on the clock face also go in the opposite direction?
5. On a straight and narrow country road, the telephone lines look like theyre connected by a line of *T*s.
6. Don't use ampersands (&s) in formal writing; spell out all *and*s.
7. Jonah counted 21 *like*s in the girls' brief conversation.
8. "Do yknow each other already?" Ahmed asked.

Write contractions for the following words.

1. do not don't
2. she is ______
3. should not ______
4. I am ______
5. were not ______
6. you are ______
7. I have ______
8. he would ______
9. I would ______
10. will not ______
11. should have ______
12. it will ______

Extend: Write three sentences in which you use a contraction, the plural of a letter, and the plural of a number.

Apostrophes to Form Possessives 1

The possessive form of a singular noun is usually created by adding an apostrophe and an *s*. Turn to 628.2 in *Write Source* for examples.

Add the missing apostrophes in the following sentences.

1. The Newfoundland's reputation as a rescue dog is legendary.
2. This unusual breeds thick, oily coat and massive frame help keep it warm, even in freezing water.
3. One of the Newfoundlands—or "Newfs"—most interesting traits is its webbed feet.
4. This canine lifeguards distinguished history begins off Canadas east coast in the 1700s.
5. Before life preservers existed, every good fishermans boat had a Newf aboard, just in case a crew members swimming skills proved to be insufficient.
6. The breeds instincts are so strong that even a Newfoundland puppy will circle swimmers, hoping to bring them to land.
7. My neighbors Newfoundland often tries to rescue me in our swimming pool—even if I don't need saving.
8. Sir Edwin Landseers Newf had black and white spots and became famous for its lifesaving prowess; today, black and white Newfs are all called Landseers.
9. One of the Newfoundlands canine relatives is the Chesapeake Bay retriever.
10. The Chessies head is wide like a Newfs.
11. Its hunting ability makes it a hunters dream dog.

Extend: Write several sentences describing the characteristics of a specific breed of animal. Correctly punctuate possessives with apostrophes.

Apostrophes to Form Possessives 2

To create the possessive form of most singular nouns, add an apostrophe and the letter *s*. To create the possessive of a plural noun that already ends in *s*, usually just add an apostrophe. Turn to 628.2–628.3 in *Write Source* for further details and examples.

Write the possessive form for each of the following words.

1. sister-in-law *sister-in-law's*
2. sister ____________
3. nobody ____________
4. students ____________
5. grass ____________
6. jack-in-the-box ____________
7. classes ____________
8. tomorrow ____________

Insert the missing elements—either an apostrophe or an apostrophe and an s—in each noun that should be possessive in the following sentences.

1. The elderly sisters own their home together, so they carved "Emma and Sally's Home Sweet Home" into a wooden sign near their front door.
2. A months worth of rain had fallen overnight.
3. Oliver envied this man-about-towns unlimited energy.
4. Tess puppy had an allergic reaction to an immunization.
5. The trade-ins values were grossly underestimated.
6. It's anybodys guess what will happen next.
7. Zara and Justine voices could be heard above the roar of the crowd.
8. Williams sponge football was confiscated by the teacher.
9. All of Mr. Smiths newspapers were scattered in the yard.
10. I'll be staying at my aunt and uncles house this weekend.

Extend: Using apostrophes to show possession, write a sentence about each of these statements: (1) Dan and Jan own a taco stand together. (2) Ike and Mike each have a new bike. (3) Jack and Jill walk up their hill.

Avoiding Awkward Apostrophes

Sometimes using possessive forms can lead to awkward writing. When that happens, it's usually best to reword the sentence and simply eliminate the troublesome apostrophes.

Awkward: **We want to honor everyone's mothers' memories on Mother's Day.**

Better: **We want to honor the memories of all mothers on Mother's Day.**

Rewrite the following sentences to eliminate the underlined awkward apostrophes.

1. We went to the airport to pick up Lois and Travis's father's luggage.

   We went to the airport to pick up the luggage belonging to Lois and Travis's father.

2. All youth group members' and friends' gifts will be placed in the hall.

3. Morris's and Doris's three-ring binders' rings were bent.

4. The rainstorm damaged my sister's band's speakers.

5. The fire destroyed all of my brother's football team's equipment.

6. The carpenters' and the electrician's noises were deafening.

Extend: Create five awkward sentences in which the possessive forms "pile up." Exchange papers with a classmate and rewrite each other's examples.

Review: Apostrophes

Write the possessive form or the contraction for the underlined words.

mother of the bride's

1. The mother of the bride dress was flowered and purple.

2. The bridesmaids dresses had the same designs but in different colors.

3. We forgot to order the groomsmen boutonnieres.

4. A broken ankle ruined Ross chance to win the 110-meter hurdles.

5. Coretta and Maynard personal achievements inspired their daughters.

6. Coretta and Maynard marriage has survived many hardships.

7. Jared gave two weeks notice when he quit his job.

8. Do not allow the words *cannot* and *will not* to dominate your life.

9. The new display case glass front was broken.

10. Be sure to wake me at seven oclock.

11. New York City skyline is instantly recognizable.

12. The girls and boys tennis teams have excellent records.

13. It is always somebody else fault.

14. Joey did not think the interviewer had read his résumé.

15. "Top o the mornin" is an Irish saying meaning "good morning."

16. Venus, Mercury, and Earth orbits are smaller than Mars orbit.

17. All her brothers and sisters-in-law children were at the reunion. (*Brothers* and *sisters-in-law* are plural.)

Quotation Marks with Dialogue 1

Place quotation marks before and after the words of a direct quotation. Use single quotation marks to punctuate a quotation within a quotation. Study the chart below to review where to place punctuation marks when they are used with quotation marks.

Placement of Punctuation		
	Inside of Quotation Marks	Outside of Quotation Marks
comma	✔	
period	✔	
colon		✔
semicolon		✔
question mark & exclamation point	✔ (when it punctuates the quotation)	✔ (when it punctuates the sentence)

Insert quotation marks where they are needed in the dialogue below. Also insert any other necessary punctuation.

Stop said the man who was in charge of the bridge. He leaned into the car and continued, I have a small herd of cattle almost ready to use this bridge. They'll be coming around the curve over there any second. Do you mind waiting a bit

No, no, of course not Dad said We'll be happy to wait

Good bloke the man said as he withdrew his torso My thanks to you

Dad and I exchanged glances. Do you think this would ever happen in America I asked.

Doubtful. Quite doubtful he said. I think they'd spend a million putting a cattle pass under the river. He continued Then the taxes would go up and the cattle would be sold to pay the taxes and the cattle pass . . .

About this time, we heard shouting: Keep movin' there! Go, girl

Cattle and the men driving them passed on both sides of the car. One curious cow stopped and stuck her head in the window Moooooo, she said.

Do you think she wants a ride I asked.

Quotation Marks with Dialogue 2

Direct quotations are enclosed in quotation marks. (*"He's smart," Jan said.*) Indirect quotations are not. (*Jan said he's smart.*) For punctuation guidelines, turn to 632.1–632.2 in *Write Source.*

Insert quotation marks where they are needed in the sentences below. If a quotation is indirect, edit the sentence to make it a direct quotation, adding commas, end punctuation, and capital letters as necessary.

1. When my mother asked me[, "Why didn't you] ~~why I didn't~~ come straight home[?"] I replied, ["]Well, when I got to the corner, there was a sign that said, 'DETOUR! BRIDGE IS OUT'!["]
2. When Lauren said that Shaq is her favorite basketball player, Lianna replied, I don't have a favorite since Michael doesn't play any longer.
3. Easing the boat into the small cove, Mitchell remarked, We should catch some nice fish here.
4. Collin said he'd rather have a pickup truck than a sports car.
5. If you want to see a beautiful part of the United States, she mused, Vermont in October is breathtaking.
6. The fire chief said that we should test our smoke alarms at least once a year to be sure they work properly.
7. The veterinarian told us that if a dog and cat are raised in the same household, they usually get along with each other quite well.
8. I don't want to bother you, Pete whispered, but may I borrow a pencil?
9. When Emily got a flat tire, she told her father she could fix it herself.
10. Several of you have been chosen for achievement awards, announced Mr. Stevens, and you should be very proud of yourselves.

Extend: Using actual or imagined dialogue, write a phone conversation between you and a friend.

Quotation Marks with Dialogue 3

Turn to 632.1–634.1 in *Write Source*.

Insert quotation marks in the passages below. Insert any missing commas as well.

1. In a review of a Canadian Brass concert, a *Washington Post* critic wrote What this amazing group of brass players achieved in their performance was absolutely unique. They inspired equal measures of laughter and admiration from the packed house.

2. The first three things you lose when you get older, she said, are your memory and—I forget the other two.

3. Tell me where it hurts, said the doctor.

4. In a letter from 1789, Thomas Jefferson wrote The execution of the laws is more important than the making of them.

5. When Dad saw us milling around in the kitchen, he said Don't forget the old proverb, Too many cooks spoil the broth.

6. Did you really just say, I love weasels? Margaret asked Phong.

7. And then, said Lilly, reading from a collection of twisted tales, Rapunzel exclaimed Thanks for stopping! And she threw her résumé to the prince.

8. Something my mother impressed upon me as a simple truth has always stuck with me: No one ever said life is fair.

9. Yes, my mother also frequently said, Who promised you a rose garden?

10. Nobody, said Roberto. I'm talking about planting vegetables.

Extend: Quote a passage from a newspaper article or an editorial that already contains a quotation. Use single and double quotation marks correctly.

Italics (Underlining) & Quotation Marks

Quotation marks are used with certain titles, such as the names of songs, poems, and short stories. Italics (or underlining) are used with the titles of longer works, such as books, magazines, and full-length plays, as well as for the names of ships and aircraft, foreign words and phrases, and other uses. Turn to 636.1–636.5 in *Write Source.*

Add underlining and quotation marks (single and double) where they are needed.

1. Rashad thoroughly enjoyed A Connecticut Yankee in King Arthur's Court, a novel by Mark Twain.
2. Rosa used the Dr. Seuss book If I Ran the Zoo for her speech project.
3. Ben said, I have never read Rolling Stone magazine.
4. I think Jim Carrey's most creative film was The Mask, observed Shawna.
5. My favorite episode of The Simpsons is called Lisa's Sax—at least I think that's the title, answered Chris.
6. Roberta shook her head and replied, My story is not Shortcakes; it's Short Takes!
7. My father reads the New York Times, but my mother prefers the Wall Street Journal.
8. Mother wants desperately to see the opera Murder in the Cathedral by Pizzetti, but Father isn't all that interested.
9. The Beatles' album Abbey Road includes both Come Together and Something.
10. When did the space shuttle Endeavor take off?
11. Lev wants to attend a seminar called You, Too, Can Get Rich Quick!
12. I bought the video Barney Teaches Numbers for my nephew.
13. Mom picked up a pamphlet, Your Skin Is Changing, at the doctor's office.

Extend: Write sentences that name your favorite track on a CD, your favorite article in any magazine, and your favorite chapter in a novel (or your favorite short story or poem in an anthology).

Review: Quotation Marks & Italics (Underlining)

Insert quotation marks or underlining where necessary.

1. <u>I Love Lucy</u> (television program)
2. Lucy Cries Wolf (television episode)
3. Lohengrin (opera)
4. Acer saccharum (scientific name)
5. Chicken Soup for the Soul (book)
6. The Gift of the Magi (short story)
7. Chicago Tribune (newspaper)
8. Immigrant Saga (magazine article)
9. I Have a Dream (speech)
10. I'm Henry the Eighth, I Am (song)
11. Caged Bird (poem)
12. Common Sense (pamphlet)
13. War of the Worlds (radio episode)
14. Marbury v. Madison (legal case)
15. Burns and Allen (radio program)
16. ciao (Italian greeting)
17. Little Women (novel)
18. Time (magazine)
19. A Telegram (book chapter)
20. Nutcracker Suite (ballet)
21. This Little Piggy (nursery rhyme)
22. Henry VIII (play)
23. Sound of Music (movie)
24. Sound of Music (CD)

Insert quotation marks or underlining where necessary in the following sentences.

1. In the Gettysburg Address, President Lincoln began, Four score and seven years ago . . .
2. American Girl magazine also publishes the pamphlet Daughters, which gives advice to parents of teenage girls.
3. I like the lesson in Aesop's story The Town Mouse and the Country Mouse that states Better beans and bacon in peace than cakes and ale in fear.
4. The musical Cats is based on T. S. Elliot's Old Possum's Book of Practical Cats; two of the cats are called Mungojerrie and Rumpelteazer.

Punctuation Used in Research Papers

Insert the necessary punctuation in these sentences from student research papers. See page 424, 632.3, 634.1, 634.3, 636.2, 638.4, and page 642 in *Write Source.*

1. Many school children used to begin their school day by saying I pledge allegiance to the flag.
2. Don't point a finger—lend a hand is good advice given by Bits & Pieces magazine.
3. In the movie Hello, Dolly!, Dolly Levi's statement to the cantankerous miser Horace Vandergelder It's no use arguing; I've made up your mind, illustrates the lively humor of this Jewish shadchen, or matchmaker.
4. Roses are red Violets are blue Sugar is sweet And will rot your teeth, too.
5. The Milwaukee Journal-Sentinel contained a recipe in the food section entitled Beans & Barley Tofu Scrambler.
6. Baseball player Albert Ortiz was a celebrity contestant playing for charity on the TV game show Who Wants to Be a Millionaire?
7. In her book Gandhi author Olivia Coolidge writes Once more his carriage was dragged through the streets; he was pelted with flowers and followed by joyful crowds crying, Gandhi! Gandhi!
8. In the movie Casablanca, Humphrey Bogart's character never says Play it again, Sam; instead, Ingrid Bergman says Play it, Sam. Play As Time Goes By.
9. In Camryn Manheim's book, Wake Up, I'm Fat!, the actress goes through a series of what she calls reality checks during the Emmy award nomination process.

Shorten the following quotation, using an ellipsis; then answer the questions.

> **To me it [the Mona Lisa] was merely a serene and subdued face, and there an end. There might be more in it, but I could not find it. The complexion was bad; in fact, it was not even human; there are no people that color.**
> **—Mark Twain, *Europe and Elsewhere*, "Down the Rhone"**

1. ______________________________

____

____

2. Why are brackets used in the quotation? ______________________________

3. Why is *Europe and Elsewhere* italicized and "Down the Rhone" enclosed in quotation marks? ______________________________

____

Review pages 437–438 in *Write Source*. Add necessary punctuation to the following references following the APA documentation style.

1. Bureau of Transportation Safety. 2004. Wisconsin alcohol traffic facts book Madison WI Wisconsin Department of Transportation ***(tech report)***

2. Childers J. & Childers D. 1996 The white-haired girl New York St. Martin's Press ***(two or more authors)***

3. Time-Life Books (2001) *Incredible Creatures* Richmond VA Author ***(corporate group author)***

4. Regional Fed banks in February begin discount-rate push 2000 May 1 Wall Street Journal p A16 ***(unsigned newspaper article)***

5. Colton K., & Brodman, J Eds. (1996) The Grolier library of international biographies Vol 9 Visual artists Danbury CT Philip Lief Group ***(edited work in a series)***

MLA Style

The Modern Language Association (MLA) has established the most popular style for documenting research papers in the humanities. Turn to pages 429–438 in *Write Source.*

Cite each source below as it would appear in an MLA-style reference list.

1. A magazine article by Deirdre Van Dyk entitled "Crossing the Virtual Street" in the January 10, 2005, issue of *Time* magazine on page 82.

   Van Dyk, Deirdre. "Crossing the Virtual Street." Time 10 Jan. 2005: 82. Print.

2. A personal interview. (Make up the information, being sure to include the name of the person interviewed and the date of the interview.)

   ____

3. A book by Mirta Ojito entitled *Finding Manana: A Memoir of Cuban Exodus* published by Penguin Press in New York, NY, in 2005.

   ____

   ____

4. "Six Misfits Test Wits on Bigger Platform," a theater review by Charles Isherwood of a play entitled *25th Annual Putnam County Spelling Bee* by Rachel Sheinkin appearing in the *New York Times* on May 3, 2005.

   ____

   ____

   ____

5. A CD recorded by Bill Staines called *Journey Home*, produced by Red House Records in 2004.

   ____

6. An article entitled "10th Planet Discovered" appearing on the *NASA Science News* Web site dated July 29, 2005. Viewed on August 2, 2010.

   ____

   ____

   ____

APA Style

For papers in science, social science, and social studies, the American Psychological Association (APA) style is often used. Turn to pages 437–438 in *Write Source.*

Review the notes below. For each example, write the corresponding entry that would appear in an APA-style reference list.

1. An unsigned newspaper article on page A4 in *The Wall Street Journal* on August 2, 2005. The title of the article is "EPA Will Order Cuts of Plants' Pollution."

EPA will order cuts of plants' pollution. (2005, August 2).

The Wall Street Journal, p. A4.

2. A single work named "The Ice: A Journey to Antarctica," written by Stephen J. Payne, appearing on pages 649–652 in an anthology (*American Sea Writing: A Literary Anthology,* edited by Peter Neill and published in 2000 by Book News in Portland, Oregon).

____

____

____

3. A book by Peter Jackson, entitled *The Mongols and the West, 1221–1410.* It was published by Harlow in England, in 2005.

____

____

4. An online article entitled "There Goes the Neighborhood" written by Fen Montaigne. The exact duplicate of the article was originally published in *Audubon* magazine in 2000.

____

____

Extend: Write an APA-style reference entry for a chapter from one of your textbooks.

Pretest: Capitalization

Cross out each lowercase letter that should be capitalized. Write the correction above it.

in january of 2000, uncle walter and aunt eunice from the midwest went on a cruise through the panama canal. my uncle said that ever since he took latin american history 101 in college (back in the dark ages, no doubt), he has been fascinated by this central american landmark.

the panama canal crosses the isthmus of panama, creating a direct passage between the atlantic ocean and the pacific ocean. It extends from cristobal on limón bay, an arm of the caribbean sea, to balboa on the bay of panama. with a length of 50 miles, a minimum width of 500 feet, and a minimum depth of 41 feet, it has been called the "eighth wonder of the world." without a doubt, it is one of the greatest engineering feats of all time, right up there with the great wall of china, the pyramids in Egypt, the akashi kaikyo bridge in japan, and the petronas towers in malaysia.

hernán cortés, the spanish conqueror of mexico, may have been the first to suggest that a canal be cut from east to west across the narrowest part of central america. some of the early explorers suggested building a canal across nicaragua, but the credit for suggesting the panamanian route goes to charles v of the holy roman empire, who ordered a survey in 1523. nothing substantial happened until the nineteenth century, when a german scientist, alexander von humboldt, wrote a book that sparked new interest in the issue. then gold was discovered in california (now known as the golden state), and people wanted to go to the american west as fast as possible. they decided a canal would be perfect, but still nothing happened.

late in the nineteenth century, an international company and the french company that built the suez canal became interested in the project, but they both went bankrupt. it was starting to look as if no one would ever succeed in getting the canal built.

the u.s. congress created the isthmus canal commission to look into recommending a route. they negotiated with colombia (then panama's owner) to buy a six-mile-wide strip of land across the isthmus, but the colombian senate vetoed the deal. four years later, panama won its independence from colombia, and the new government of panama signed the hay-bunau-varilla treaty. president theodore roosevelt appointed colonel george w. goethals in 1907 to head the project, and by 1914, just as ww 1 was beginning, the canal was completed.

in 1977, when jimmy carter was president, the united states of america and the republic of panama signed the panama canal treaty. that began a process to turn the canal over to panama. a neutrality treaty was also signed in order to keep the waterway open for the benefit of all nations. at noon on december 31, 1999, a new panamanian agency called the panama canal authority assumed full control of the waterway.

if you'd like to read more about this subject, try these books: *path between the seas* by david mccullough or *panama and the united states* by edmund lindop.

Capitalization 1

Remembering to capitalize the first word of a sentence is pretty easy. The rules for capitalizing the other words in a sentence—from parts of the country to an upcoming high school event—are a little trickier. Turn to pages 648, 650, and 652 in *Write Source* and use a dictionary.

Cross out every lowercase letter in the following sentences that should be capitalized and write the correction above it. Some sentences do not contain errors.

1. Just as an alarm started ringing, andrew came out of the building yelling, "help! There's a fire in the stockroom!"

2. Here's my favorite quotation from shakespeare: "to thine own self be true."

3. My new computer is coming october 24 (at least I think that's the date).

4. The declaration of independence does not start with these words: "four score and seven years ago . . ."

5. No one (other than me) has the combination to my locker.

6. Tonight, roger, tracy, and I will use the computer to look at the nasa web site, while the rest of you go to the library to research halley's comet.

7. Does d.d.s. stand for "doctor of dental surgery"? (maybe it means "doctor of dental science"; I'm not sure.)

8. I've never seen mom so flustered. She sputtered for a couple of seconds before she was able to reply, "well, if that's the way you want it, fine!"

9. Have you (or anyone else on the team, as far as you know) talked about who will be the team captain?

10. Did you know that your dad invited aunt lori to come visit us?

11. I can tell you this much: the european delegates are at the white house.

12. My friend Marwan is a muslim.

Extend: Write a paragraph about a school situation. Include a sentence in parentheses and a sentence following a colon. Capitalize words appropriately.

Capitalization 2

This exercise focuses on capitalizing proper nouns. Turn to pages 648, 650, and 652 in *Write Source* and use a dictionary.

Write **a sentence using each type of proper noun requested.**

1. A country, a city, and a person's name: *My friend Ella lived in Geneva, Switzerland, for several years.*
2. A state and a national monument or park: ______
3. Two government organizations: ______
4. A sports team and a city: ______
5. A political party and a building: ______
6. A band name and a location: ______
7. A street name and a type of car: ______
8. A course title, a person's title, and a last name: ______
9. A movie title and a first name: ______

Extend: List three proper nouns for each of the following: (1) abbreviations, (2) buildings, (3) names of people, (4) organizations, (5) countries, and (6) public areas.

Capitalization 3

Proper nouns take many forms. This exercise concentrates on place names, directions, and all types of geography. Turn to page 648 and 650.4 in *Write Source* and use a dictionary.

Cross out each letter in the following personal essay that is incorrectly capitalized or lowercased—and write the correction above it.

Last summer my family embarked on a driving tour of the united states. We started in the northeast—maine, to be exact—and worked our way South and then West. My favorite part of the journey's first leg was the east coast. I loved gazing out the window of our car at the Atlantic ocean. I also enjoyed new york city, where manhattan's towering maze of buildings left me awestruck.

After a stop in washington, d.c., we headed south to atlanta, georgia, and then spent a short time on florida's beaches on the gulf of mexico. From there, it took only a day or two to reach new orleans and a spectacular view of the mississippi delta. Our trip to the west really gave me a better idea of the vastness of the United States. The fields and plains seemed to stretch on forever, especially in texas. My father informed me that the states immediately North of texas look similar—oklahoma, kansas, nebraska, and the dakotas.

In the West, the highlight was the grand canyon, a wonder carved in rock by the unceasing waters of the colorado river. It is easily one of the most impressive sights in all of north america, possibly even the world. After a brief stop in las vegas—another kind of wonder entirely—we took a quick drive on interstate 15 to los angeles. then we headed up the west coast, all the way through the redwood forests to rainy seattle. What a trip!

Extend: Write a short travelogue—real or imagined (maybe about the return trip from Seattle to Maine). Include directions and the names of actual places, such as towns, natural wonders, and tourist attractions.

Review: Capitalization

Cross out each letter that should be capitalized. Write the correction above it.

1. “Is the eiffel tower located farther north than the statue of liberty?” the student asked.
2. Which of the great lakes is the largest (as measured by surface area)?
3. the ancient greeks believed that everything in the world was made up of the four classic elements: earth, air, fire, and water.
4. uncle steve told me he would be happy to live in the midwest or the west.
5. He then added that he would also be happy in the eastern or southern united states.
6. My aunt and I were on our way to smith’s department store when she realized she’d forgotten her purse.
7. Suddenly, she made an illegal u-turn—right in front of officer ramirez.
8. I went to see the polka kings in new york’s central park with my mom and dad. (luckily I didn’t see anyone I knew!)
9. our college football team is taking on the washington wildcats on friday night.
10. A blast from a ufo tore apart the empire state building less than halfway through the movie *independence day.*
11. Last september I bought a tommy hilfiger t-shirt, and by early spring I had grown so much I had to give it to my little sister.
12. Dallas drives a four-wheel-drive truck that he bought in the south.
13. The Denver broncos are my favorite team in the national football league.
14. This past winter I took art history 102 at a community college.

Numbers & Abbreviations 1

Some numbers are written out; others are presented as numerals. Some abbreviations are always acceptable; others are not acceptable in formal writing. For details, see 658.1–661.1 in your *Write Source* textbook and use a dictionary.

Underline each abbreviation, word, or number that would be incorrect or unacceptable in formal writing. Write the correction above it.

United States

1. The exploration of outer space by the U.S. is the responsibility of the National Aeronautics and Space Administration (N.A.S.A.).
2. N.A.S.A. headquarters are located in Washington, D.C.
3. Here is the exact address: 400 Maryland Ave., Wash., D.C. 20546.
4. Last semester, 7 students wrote to N.A.S.A. for info.
5. After a decade of moon exploration with space probes, 2 U.S. astronauts landed on the lunar surface on July twentieth, 1969.
6. A total of 6 two-man crews of Amer. astronauts landed on the moon between nineteen-sixty-nine and nineteen-seventy-two.
7. They returned to earth with more than seven-hundred-ninety lbs. of moon rocks.
8. Some of the craters on the moon's surface are fifty-six miles wide.
9. The moon is roughly 1/4, or 25%, the size of the earth.
10. Earth has one moon, Mars has two, and Jupiter has 16.
11. A total eclipse of the moon took place on Oct. twenty-eighth, 1985.
12. Ken needs 6 11-inch straws to complete his model of a futuristic spaceship.
13. A light-year is a unit of length equal to the distance that light travels in 1 year.
14. This distance is about five trillion eight hundred seventy-eight billion miles.

Extend: Write a paragraph about the supplies you would need for a building project of your choice, noting prices and measurements.

Numbers & Abbreviations 2

If you are unsure whether you should write out a number, turn to page 658 in *Write Source*. For information on abbreviations, initialisms, and acronyms, turn to pages 660–662.

Underline each error in the sentences below and write the correction above. Consider this formal writing. Not all the sentences need correction.

1. Tina's mom is only five ft. tall. *(feet)*
2. My uncle lives near Hilton Head Island in SC.
3. Troy's dog keeps waking him up at 4 o'clock a.m.
4. Only students between the ages of nine and 13 are accepted into the program.
5. Twelve greyhounds take part in each of the eight races.
6. We found that eighty-five % of our class has brown eyes.
7. Mister Cosford plays the drums in a jazz band.
8. Many people like to drive from Chicago to California on Route Sixty-Six.
9. Turn to p. ten in your P.E. manual.
10. The highest recorded temperature at the South Pole, only a few °'s above zero on the F scale, occurred Dec. 27, 1978.

Label each acronym with an *A* and each initialism with an *I*. Write out what the acronym or initialism stands for.

A **1.** scuba *self-contained underwater breathing apparatus*

_____ **2.** CEO _____

_____ **3.** HIV _____

_____ **4.** MADD _____

_____ **5.** SWAT _____

Extend: Clip out a newspaper article that includes a lot of figures. Compare clippings with a classmate and discuss how newspaper style differs from formal writing.

Pretest: Plurals & Spelling

Underline each misspelled word below and write the correction above it.

1. When all of you high school seniors are no longer under your mothers' and
roofs
fathers' rooves, your lifes will be different in many ways.

2. While some of you will be at home next year, many of you will be continueing your education at colleges, universitys, and trade schools; getting jobs; or joining the armed services.

3. You will be carrying armsloads of clothing, electronic equipment, books, and other things you recieved for graduation into your new dorm rooms, apartments, and barracks.

4. While you're at it, don't forget to pack some dish's and other supplys to fill the empty shelfs in your new living quarters.

5. Here's a healthy entrée for partys, as well as for everyday menues, that you can vary in a hundred different ways.

6. Many of you may have grown up eating homemade tortillas, burritoes, or tacoes that are better for you than anything you can buy at fast-food drives-ins.

7. These ansient foods—a staple of Mexican diets for cenchuries—are both a meal and a serving utensel.

8. You can buy them at supermarkets or at Mexican bakerys where they are baked fresh dayly, or you can make your own.

9. Sauté ground beef and chop fresh tomatos, peppers, olives, and lettuce, plus plenty of oniones or scallions.

10. Some people say pinto beens are preferrable to black beans; luckily, you can buy canned varietys of both rather inexpensivly.

11. If you are realy adventurous, try making tortillas the way Mexican housewifes did in the olden days.

12. The basic resipe for making tortillas manualy starts like this: Mix one part cornmeal with two parts water (and a splash of lime juice).

13. You may not appreshiate why lime is a cruical element in tortillas.

14. Lime helps corn release niacin, an important vitamin whose absense causes pellagra, a nasty gastrointestinal diseas that is endemic in some parts of the world.

15. Lime also boosts the tortillas' calcium content, esential for strong bones and exellent, steady nerves.

16. My nieghbor makes her tortillas from scratch, and I must admit that the taste and texture are unforgetable.

17. I will probly never attempt to make tortillas from scratch myself, but I am becomeing very handy with the can opener that my two sister-in-laws gave me as a joke for my birthday.

Plurals 1

Creating the plural form of some nouns is not a simple matter of adding an *s*. Turn to the rules at 654.1–656.4 in *Write Source* and use a dictionary.

Write the plural of each word below. Then explain the corresponding rule or rules.

1. ax *axes* ____________ ash ____________

hunch ____________ class ____________

Rule: ____________

____

2. potato ____________ patio ____________

zoo ____________ gecko ____________

Rule: ____________

____

____

____

3. spoonful ____________ boxful ____________

Rule: ____________

____

____

4. five-year-old ____________ sister-in-law ____________

attorney-at-law ____________ go-getter ____________

Rule: ____________

____

Extend: Create a list of singular nouns—two for each rule above. (Don't duplicate the examples on this page.) Exchange papers with a classmate and write the plurals for the words in one another's list.

Plurals 2

Creating the plural form of some nouns is not a simple matter of adding an *s.* Turn to the rules at 654.1–656.4 in *Write Source* and use a dictionary.

Write the plural of each word below. Then explain the corresponding rule or rules.

1. city cities ______ essay ______
   cowboy ______ destiny ______
   Rule: ______
   ______
   ______

2. person ______ datum ______
   mouse ______ octopus ______
   Rule: ______
   ______
   ______

3. E ______ 76 ______ oh ______
   & ______ Δ ______ hello ______
   Rule: ______
   ______
   ______

4. thief ______ life ______
   loaf ______ fife ______
   Rule: ______
   ______
   ______
   ______

Spelling 1

Here's a common spelling rule: Write *i* before *e* except after *c*, or when sounded like *a* as in *neighbor* and *weigh*. For exceptions, turn to 664.1 in *Write Source* and use a dictionary.

Underline each misspelled word below and write the correct spelling above it.

achievement

1. The suspension bridge across the bay was a great acheivement.
2. DeWayne thought the coffee had too much caffiene.
3. The conveneince-store casheir's conscience prevented him from being decietful.
4. The foreign currency was counterfiet.
5. My eight-year-old neice, Ruby, tends to get into mischeif.
6. The feirce wind lowered the efficeincy of the old windows.
7. Is your liesure time so important that you neglect your personal hygeine?
8. Uncle Silas's greif over the accident was percieved as extreme.
9. My patience was tried during the breif interview.
10. It was Nori's beleif that she would recieve a piece of pie after dinner.
11. The Arab shiek was a major financier.
12. Sometimes I think men and women are different spieces entirely.
13. The laws for search and siezure relate to the Fourth Amendment.
14. The surviellance camera caught the theif on tape.
15. Protien is a necessary nutrient.
16. I think my anxiety will be releived if I take a long vacation.
17. The yeild on the one-year certificate of deposit is 5.2 percent.

Extend: From the list of commonly misspelled words in *Write Source* (pages 666–667), select three to five *ie* or *ei* words that do not appear above. Use the words in sentences.

Spelling 2

Spelling rules can help you add suffixes to words correctly. Turn to 664.2–664.4 in *Write Source* and use a dictionary.

Underline each misspelled word and write the correction above it.

1. It is advisable
   adviseable to take a psychology course if you are pursueing a career in advertising.
2. The attorneyes insist that this legal document is changeable.
3. Your sillyness is wholely unacceptible.
4. Naturaly, I am gratefull that you stoped snoring.
5. Pablo found his handheld computer not merely valuble, but indispenseable.
6. In remembrance of her grandfather, Lu planed a small gathering of his closest friends and relatives.
7. Reggie cooly stepped into the bus, forgetting there was a very noticeable grease mark on his face.
8. Great-aunt Lil has tryed to fill her life with remarkable journies.
9. By not getting enough sleep, you make yourself susceptable to common illnesses.
10. Dora was typing an expense report that, unfortunatly, was full of unjustifyable expenditures.
11. "This model also gets exceptionaly good gas milage," explained the manufacturer's representive.
12. Apply a prepareation of baking soda and laundery soap to the stain before washing; that will probabley take care of it.

Extend: One of the most annoying things about the English language is all the exceptions to the rules. Review the list of commonly misspelled words in your textbook (pages 666–667), and find two exceptions to the rules about adding suffixes.

Spelling 3

This exercise features commonly misspelled words. For help, turn to pages 666–667 in *Write Source* and use a dictionary.

Circle the misspelled word in each pair below and write the correction in the blank.

1. absess, vigilance abscess
2. intercede, especially ______
3. criticisim, partial ______
4. seperate, gracious ______
5. debtor, maintenence ______
6. lovable, lovelly ______
7. temperture, innocence ______
8. yeild, thorough ______
9. religious, unaminous ______
10. questionaire, knowledge ______
11. livelyhood, humorous ______
12. fourty, fourth ______
13. essential, aquired ______
14. catastrophy, commission ______
15. surely, ordinarly ______
16. parallell, naive ______
17. unnecessary, manuever ______
18. wreckage, offence ______
19. luxury, priviledge ______
20. hemorrhage, embarass ______

Extend: From the list above, choose three to five words you don't feel confident using. Look them up in a dictionary and write a sentence containing each one.

Spelling 4

This exercise features commonly misspelled words. For help, turn to pages 666–667 in *Write Source* and use a dictionary.

Circle each correctly spelled word below. Only one word in each group is correct.

1. allowence, alowance, allowance
2. irridescent, iridescent, irridesent
3. disasterous, disastrous, desastrous
4. assosiate, asociate, associate
5. desirable, desirible, desireable
6. rythem, rythm, rhythm
7. labratory, laboratory, labortory
8. shedule, schedul, schedule
9. exagerate, exaggerate, exaggirate
10. eligible, eligable, elagible
11. hemorrhage, hemmorhage, hemmorage
12. assinement, assignment, assignement
13. infered, inferred, infurred
14. guidance, guideance, guiddance
15. incidently, incidentaly, incidentally
16. courageous, couragous, couragious
17. fourtunate, fortuneate, fortunate
18. perceive, percieve, perseive
19. bountyful, bountiful, bountifull
20. unforgetable, unforgetible, unforgettable

Extend: Write sentences using three to five of the words above that trouble you.

Review: Plurals and Spelling

Underline the correct word in each parenthetical pair in the sentences below.

1. Her religious *(beliefs, believes)* require her to wear a *(veil, viel)* in public.
2. Yes, it is *(likly, likely)* that I will stop for *(groceries, grocereys)* on my way home.
3. A degree in chemistry would be *(advantagous, advantageous)* in the *(field, feild)* of bioengineering.
4. Only *(women, wimen)* are permitted to join *(sorority's, sororities)*.
5. Susan pondered the best way to tell Jarvis he would be *(transfered, transferred)* to Greenland by the year's end; none of the possible *(approachs, approaches)* seemed ideal.
6. Ian was *(accumulating, accumulateing)* a vast collection of action *(videoes, videos)*.
7. Naomi was *(hopping, hoping)* the nomination committee would think she was *(qualifyed, qualified)*.
8. Mom thought the tempera paints were still *(useable, usable)*, so she set out two *(bowlsful, bowlfuls)* for the children.
9. Mold, mushrooms, and yeast are all *(fungus, fungi)* and are *(usualy, usually)* classified as plants.
10. *(Studeying, Studying)* grammar may seem tedious, but *(personally, personelly)* I don't find it half as tedious as listening to mangled English.
11. *(Unfortunately, Unfortunatly)*, we can't make it to the game.
12. The *(thieves, thiefs)* made a *(collosal, colossal)* blunder when they asked a policeman for directions.

13. It never *(occured, occurred)* to her that the birds might be wild *(turkeys, turkies).*

14. My *(friend, freind)* and I are considered the entertainers in our *(familys, families).*

15. My nose is so stuffy that I'm having trouble *(breatheing, breathing).*

16. The salesperson gave Basha full *(assureance, assurance)* that the service technician could stop the leak in her *(basement, basment).*

17. The nutritionist *(refered, referred)* Ellen to a health-food store for a *(preparation, prepareation)* of alfalfa, gingko, and vitamin B.

18. Ramón's *(inquirey, inquiry)* into the *(mysteryous, mysterious)* happenings led him nowhere.

19. A chorus of enthusiastic *(yes's, yeses)* greeted the question, "Are we *(equiped, equipped)* to handle this situation?"

20. Warships are sometimes called *(man-of-wars, men-of-war).*

21. It can be *(extremely, extremly)* difficult for *(fameous, famous)* people to live a normal life.

22. Because of their frequent overseas *(journeys, journies),* they have been *(omitted, omited)* from our mailing list.

23. There have been a lot of *(deers, deer)* in our backyard lately.

24. We thought that *(surely, surly)* he must have realized the oil was *(inflamable, inflammable).*

Pretest: Using the Right Word

Circle the correct word in each set of choices in the essay below.

Whether you agree with those *(who, whom)* say the 1900s spawned the most rapid changes in recorded history, you have to admit that it was an era of *(continual, continuous)* turmoil and technological progress . . . and *(its, it's)* legacy continues.

When the twentieth century began, *(less, fewer)* than 2 billion people inhabited the planet. Today, China alone has that *(amount, number)* of people. The discovery of powerful antibiotics and hybrid grains has contributed to explosive population growth. People live longer *(than, then)* ever before. As a result, government leaders struggle with demands for resources. At times, arguments *(among, between)* two nations trying to meet these demands have led to war.

The availability of vast amounts of information worldwide has changed the way governments and economies work. Now, it is *(plain, plane)* to see what is happening elsewhere in the world. At the same time, all this information is subject to manipulation and *(vary, very)* susceptible to error.

Moon visits, heart transplants, GPS devices, hybrid cars, artificial knees, and personal computers are only some of the technological advances that *(affect, effect)* people. Technology can make peoples' lives better, but it can be used for evil purposes also. Certainly, *(good, well)* national policies are important. However, we all *(bad, badly)* need to make positive *(personal, personnel)* decisions as well.

Using the Right Word 1

For help with this exercise, turn to the list of commonly misused words on pages 678 and 680 in *Write Source.*

Underline the correct word in each set of choices in the following sentences.

1. Most theaters use small safety lights to light the *(aisles, isles).*
2. Labor Day is one of many *(annual, biannual)* events in the United States.
3. Antoine's careless use of the table saw resulted in a *(bad, badly)* injured hand.
4. The members of the Central High School band were extremely pleased with the *(amount, number)* of students from area schools who attended the concert.
5. After the destructive storm had passed, volunteers searched *(among, between)* the shattered houses looking for injured people.
6. Passengers anxiously glanced at their watches, knowing that the train was *(already, all ready)* half an hour late.
7. After removing the starter motor from the truck's engine, the mechanic set the motor *(beside, besides)* his ohmmeter.
8. Ice buildup on the wings of an airplane can have an adverse *(affect, effect)* on the plane's ability to fly.
9. A good leader is willing to *(accept, except)* responsibility for mistakes that he or she has made.
10. *(Among, Between)* the foothills and the majestic mountain range, a river full of glacial silt continuously cuts its way through the wide plateau.
11. As the driver set the truck's plow down, he could tell that although this was not a record *(amount, number)* of snow, there was still a lot of work to do.

Extend: Write a sentence for each of the following words: *annual, biannual, semiannual, biennial, perennial.*

Using the Right Word 2

Turn to pages 682 and 684 in *Write Source* for help with this exercise.

Choose the correct word from the list below to fill the blanks.

brake, break; cereal, serial; chord, cord; chose, choose; complement, compliment; continual, continuous; desert, dessert; different from, different than; fewer, less

1. After two hours of piano practice before her concert, Camille took a ___break___.
2. Camille decided to play ______________ pieces than she had first planned.
3. She didn't want to eat a big meal, so she poured herself a bowl of ______________.
4. She knew there would be a ______________ reception after the concert.
5. After her snack, Camille started practicing a difficult ______________ sequence.
6. Previously, one critic had written a ______________ about her obvious hard work.
7. For this evening's concert, Camille ______________ an elegant black dress.
8. Around her neck, Camille wore a gold pendant on a blue-black ______________.
9. She wanted this concert to be ______________ all her other concerts.
10. Her practices had been ______________ for the last month—an hour each day.
11. Camille's practice paid off as her playing now took ______________ effort.
12. Before driving to the concert hall, she took a moment to ______________ a CD.
13. She released the parking ______________ and began the 20-minute trip.
14. At the concert, Camille placed a rose on the piano to ______________ her performance.
15. When she finished, the audience rewarded her with a long minute of ______________ applause.

Extend: Write a sentence for each one of the following words: *complement, desert, different than, serial.*

Using the Right Word 3

Turn to pages 686 and 688 in *Write Source* for help with this exercise.

Circle the correct word in each set of choices in the sentences below.

1. Emma has a *(flair, flare)* for choosing color combinations.
2. Jason realized that to *(insure, ensure)* his car he'd have to get a job.
3. After they jogged several miles, Sharon let her German shepherd *(lay, lie)* down and rest.
4. Caroline can *(borrow, lend)* Jay's cell phone to call her mom.
5. The ultimate goal of every Olympic athlete is to win a gold *(medal, meddle).*
6. The letter confused Evan because it seemed to *(imply, infer)* that he needed to pay an entrance fee, which he had already paid.
7. Devon dreamed about catching a pass thrown by his *(idle, idol),* quarterback James Larson.
8. Ellen was pleased to find that the program she designed worked *(good, well).*
9. Jake didn't want to *(medal, meddle),* but he told Allan about the new plan.
10. James, carefully *(lay, lie)* your wood project on the top display shelf.
11. "Josh," Wu Lee pleaded, "please *(borrow, lend)* me your portable CD player."
12. Do you think the student council will review this memo and *(imply, infer)* that students will have to pay for all extracurricular activities?
13. Our science teacher held the jaws of the baby alligator shut to *(insure, ensure)* it would not bite anyone.
14. Reading a *(good, well)* book is a great way to spend time waiting for a bus.
15. Coach Behrens was pleased that his team's schedule included an *(idle, idol)* date over the holidays.

Using the Right Word 4

Turn to pages 690 and 692 in *Write Source* for help with this exercise.

Underline each word that has been used incorrectly. Write the correction above it.

principal

1. Our principle, Mr. Slade, always reminds us to keep our priorities straight.
2. He said that it was plane to see that some students get poor grades because they don't realize that some things are more important than others.
3. Mr. Slade's favorite quote is "First of all, know what you need, and then what you want will take care of itself."
4. He reminded us that high school graduation is not just a right of passage.
5. All of the school personal agree with his philosophy.
6. These staff members go out of their way to peek the interest of the students.
7. With the wring of the first bell, the business of education begins.
8. The work is challenging and tests the metal of the students.
9. My personnel goal is to finish in the upper 10 percent of my class.
10. Although trigonometry was real difficult for me, I improved all quarter.
11. Inspired by Mr. Slade, all of us are dedicated to the principal of doing our best.
12. Before graduating, every senior must write a well-reasoned persuasive essay.
13. A peak at the list shows that almost everyone has fulfilled that requirement.
14. As graduation approaches, the next stage in life suddenly becomes real.
15. Many students have decided to order class wrings that quote the school motto: "Learning never stops."

Using the Right Word 5

Turn to pages 694 and 696 in *Write Source*.

Underline each incorrectly used word and write the correction above it.

Who's

1. Whose working on the class play this year?
2. At one time, oil refineries burned off natural gas as a waist product.
3. The gym's logbook shows that the stationery bike is the most popular piece of exercise equipment.
4. First Joel sanded the trunk, and than he applied five thin coats of varnish.
5. Kelsey and Associates just prepared the building sight for the new school.
6. The weather vain on the clock tower was hit by lightning and destroyed.
7. Sylvia wrote a letter to each of her friends using her new floral stationary.
8. Please take you're notebook with you on today's hike.
9. These students are late because they were on the bus which broke down.
10. To who did you lend the DVD?
11. Before surgery, a nurse placed an IV in a large vane in Greg's left arm.
12. In his paper, Daren decided to site a passage from *The Bridge of San Luis Rey.*
13. Does anyone know who's book this is?
14. Jose bought his favorite band's latest CD, that is sweeping the country.
15. By 3:00 p.m. tomorrow, I must know whom is planning to go see the play *Julius Caesar.*

Extend: Write a sentence for each of the following words: *who, whom, stationary,* and *which.*

Review: Using the Right Word

Underline each usage error in the personal essay below and write the correction above it.

which

In 1790, Congress formed the Coast Guard, that was the first maritime service in the United States. The initial five distinct coastal-water agencies eventually merged to form today's Coast Guard. This agency excepts responsibility for shipping inspection, fishing regulation, lighthouse keeping, and search-and-rescue operations.

Perhaps the most dramatic Coast Guard stories are those of search and rescue. These are times which test the metal of the Coast Guard because often these operations occur during real dangerous weather conditions. Rescuing survivors of sinking boats or ships is hazardous and, of course, makes the difference among life and death. Such accounts positively effect young people who want to help those in trouble. Men and women of the Coast Guard work to insure the safety of people along the coasts of this country.

One story of a sailboat battered and sinking in a storm represents the best of the Coast Guard. A brave crew rescued the personal on the boat while the helicopter in a stationery hover risked being hit by 50-foot waves. One of the guard choose to drop into the water at the rite time. If he missed the pique of the wave, he risked falling 60 feet into the trough among the waves. Once in the water, he made his way to the stricken sailboat, coaxed the people into the water, and than prepared them to be hoisted out of the water beside patiently waiting for his own turn to get back in the aircraft. The wind howled, blasting the sea to foam and pounding the helicopter, but the crew successfully completed the mission.

The work of the Coast Guard is real important. The amount of responsibilities has increased. The Coast Guard covers the Great Lakes, the East and West Coasts, and the coasts of Alaska and Hawaii. Territorial waters in the ocean now extend 200 miles from land and are under continual patrol by the Coast Guard. During some wars, Coast Guard duties were different than peacetime assignments. In fact, Coast Guard cutters complimented the navy by sinking submarines, assisting the landing of forces, and fighting against enemy surface warships.

Although their main purpose is serving the United States, men and women of the service also chose to help people from other countries. The Coast Guard knows it's principle work is protecting the coast, upholding sea laws, and helping those in danger.

Underline each usage error in the following sentences and write the correction above it. (Three sentences have no errors.)

implying

1. "Are you inferring that I should leave?" she asked angrily.
2. Please except this gift as a token of our appreciation.
3. The number of people attending the ball games has risen dramatically.
4. My new cell phone is different than my brother's cell phone.
5. The writer has all ready written his fifth novel.
6. Grandma always lies down for a nap in the afternoon.
7. The crowd hears the opening cords of the national anthem and stands up.
8. West Quoddy Head, Maine, is farther east then any other point in the United States.
9. Your new painting really compliments the room's decor.
10. That dessert was so tasty!

Proofreading Review

Test your skills as a proofreader as you read the paragraphs below. Add, remove, or change punctuation as necessary; capitalize each letter that should be capitalized; use numerals or spelled-out numbers correctly; fix spelling and usage errors; and punctuate or write out each abbreviation correctly.

~~h~~Have you ever ~~traviled~~ traveled to another country? I know from personnel experience that living abroad can be an exciting and memorable adventure when I was twelve years old my family spent 6 months in London england. We lived in a small Flat in kensington gardens, kensington gardens is close to london the financial and fashion center of England.

london is a fascinating city, it is filled with historical buildings such as the houses of parliament the british museum and st pauls cathedral moreover it is home to cultural sights such as the royal academy of arts. During our 6 month stay my family spent countless ours walking through the british museum riding the double-decker buses and retracing the steps of famous british poets and righters.

It was in London that I 1st discovered the differences between american english and the queens english. My introduction to the queens english was swift and confusing one day I started out for the british museum but I got lost looking for the train. I stopped a distinguished looking gentleman and asked him wear I might find the subway.

Subway? he asked, looking confused.

yes train. You know it goes underground . . . choo-choo, I replied.

He scratched his head, than said, Subway? Are you sure?

Yes, I replied. I know there's one nearby.

Suddenly he brightened. Ah, yes indeed, the tube.

Tube I asked.

He smiled wisely. My dear young man in england its called the tube.

Their were many other times I felt betrayed by my native language. The british say lift for elevator biscuits for cookys and bumbershoot for umbrella. In short, theirs is a very confusing english.

Although the language is confusing the weather often rainy and the food different london is a magical city. The city itself dates back to the second century. Parts of londons early city can be scene in fragments of roman brick that are visible in the walls of the tower of london. During walking tours history buffs enjoy tracing the citys development and growth these tours take you through covent garden the cheif flower and fruit market; fleet street the center of londons newspaper industry and buckingham palace where one can still witness the changing of the guard.

London is a very special city and deserves a liesurely visit. I'm glad I was able to spend this time in another country Its a time I'll never forget.

Parts of Speech Activities

The activities in this section provide a review of the different parts of speech. Most of the activities also include helpful textbook references. In addition, the **Extend** activities encourage follow-up practice of certain skills.

Pretest: Nouns

Underline all the nouns in the following sentences. (Do not underline pronouns.)

1. Most diseases strike older people, but a few are actually more common among children and young adults.
2. Eighteen million people in the United States have diabetes, and more than a tenth of them are under the age of 20.
3. When my sister Tamika was diagnosed with diabetes, she was a freshman at Winston High School, trying out for the volleyball team.
4. Besides adjusting to all the changes that high school brings, Tamika had to make big changes in her diet and lifestyle.
5. Suddenly, she had to plan her meals with great care and give herself daily shots of insulin.
6. At first Tamika rebelled and refused to follow the doctor's orders, a course that landed her in St. Luke's Hospital several times.
7. After Dr. O'Donnell, Rev. Thompson, and Grandma Wilson talked to her and let her express her feelings and fears, she got with the program.
8. This situation has been tough for everyone in our family, but in some ways we have benefited: we are all eating a better diet now.

List three nouns from the sentences above that fit the following categories.

	Proper	Abstract	Collective
1.	*Tamika*		
2.			
3.			

Types of Nouns

A noun is the name of a person, a place, a thing, or an idea. Turn to page 701 in *Write Source*. Some nouns show possession *(Jane's dress)*. Some nouns are compound *(freezing point, job-hopping)*; some of these are hyphenated, others are not. Use a dictionary.

Underline the nouns below. (Do not underline the pronouns.)

1. Lori spoke with her friend Darrell and asked him how to use a snowboard.
2. The idea intrigued her, and she wanted more information.
3. Darrell told her it wasn't an easy sport.
4. You must learn how to control the snowboard correctly and recognize your limitations.
5. Risky stunts may be exciting and look great, but they often result in injuries that bring things to a complete halt.
6. The sport puts stress on the legs and back of a snowboarder, but the hands and wrists are most likely to be injured.
7. The reason is simple: many boarders break their falls with their hands.
8. Lori wasn't afraid, so she asked Darrell to teach her.
9. He was glad to help and lent Lori some of his old equipment.
10. The thought of flying down the hills made Lori's pulse quicken.
11. She found the snowboard very awkward, but that only made her more determined to succeed.
12. The day was cold, with temperatures far below the freezing point.
13. Darrell said Lori showed natural talent on her very first attempt.
14. Tanya, a friend from school, was skiing past and stopped to watch.
15. An hour later, Tanya was learning to snowboard, too.

Extend: Select a short newspaper or magazine article and underline all the nouns.

Classes of Nouns

Nouns can be classified as (1) proper or common, (2) concrete or abstract, and (3) collective. See page 701 in *Write Source.*

Identify the classes of each noun below. Use *P* for proper or *C* for common on the first line; use *CON* for concrete or *AB* for abstract on the second line. If a noun is collective, circle it.

C CON **1.** troop

____ ____ **2.** goodness

____ ____ **3.** Sarah

____ ____ **4.** skateboard

____ ____ **5.** carrots

____ ____ **6.** Miami Beach

____ ____ **7.** peace

____ ____ **8.** crowd

____ ____ **9.** drums

____ ____ **10.** flock

____ ____ **11.** joy

____ ____ **12.** family

____ ____ **13.** Matt Damon

____ ____ **14.** carelessness

____ ____ **15.** avalanche

____ ____ **16.** group

____ ____ **17.** freedom

____ ____ **18.** brother

____ ____ **19.** dictatorship

____ ____ **20.** anger

____ ____ **21.** Nadia

____ ____ **22.** kidney

____ ____ **23.** *Mona Lisa*

____ ____ **24.** committee

____ ____ **25.** banana bread

____ ____ **26.** *Moby Dick*

Choose a proper noun from above and use it in a sentence below.

____

Choose both an abstract and a concrete noun from above and use them in a sentence.

____

____

Extend: Who hasn't heard of a herd of cows? But not many people know that a group of kangaroos is called a mob. Visit the library or the Internet and find the collective nouns for 15 different animal groups, including crows, geese, and lions.

Functions of Nouns

The chart below shows six ways to use nouns. See *Write Source* for details.

Write Source	Function	Symbol	Example
738.1	*subject*	***S***	*Burglars* steal.
702.3	*predicate noun*	***PN***	Burglars are *thieves.*
716.2	*direct object*	***DO***	Burglars steal your *possessions.*
716.2	*indirect object*	***IO***	Burglars gave *Grandpa* a scare.
732	*object of preposition*	***OP***	Burglars pried the jewels out of his *hands.*
702.3	*possessive noun*	***POS***	Burglars stole *Grandma's* jewelry.

Label the function of each underlined noun in the following sentences, using the symbols from the chart above.

POS OP

1. My brother's room is filled with books.
2. We saw a coyote in the meadow.
3. Basketball is the favorite sport of many Americans.
4. The teachers gave the seniors a lecture about irresponsibility.
5. "Irresponsibility is laziness" was one teacher's opinion.
6. The streets are packed with hundreds of cars at rush hour.
7. The capital of Alaska is Juneau.
8. That team gives spectators their money's worth!
9. The seamstress made a dress for Ms. Tomas.
10. Grandpa Gilbertson took quilting lessons.
11. The store clerk walked two miles to return the man's billfold.
12. Did Abraham Lincoln and Vincent Van Gogh live at the same time?
13. Next week Marci and Petra will throw their parents an anniversary party.
14. The architecture in this neighborhood intrigues me.

Extend: Choose one noun. Write some sentences in which you try to use this noun in all six ways listed above. Identify how the nouns function in your sentences.

Nominative, Possessive, & Objective Cases of Nouns

The chart below illustrates the three cases of nouns. Turn to 702.3 in *Write Source* for more details.

Write Source	Case	Function	Symbol	Example
738.1	Nominative	*subject*	***S***	The *car* wouldn't start.
702.3		*predicate noun*	***PN***	The car is a *lemon*.
716.2	Objective	*direct object*	***DO***	Jake drives his *car* carefully.
716.2		*indirect object*	***IO***	Jake gave *Rena* a driving lesson.
732		*object of preposition*	***OP***	He drives with both *hands*.
702.3	Possessive	*possessive noun*	***POS***	*Hannah's* driving skills are much better.

Identify the function of each underlined noun using the symbols in the chart above. In the blank provided, indicate the case of the noun: write *N* for nominative, *O* for objective, or *POS* for possessive.

____ **1.** Many different designs have been proposed for the spacecraft of tomorrow.

____ **2.** Some designs resemble the spacecraft used today, which burn chemical fuel for propulsion.

____ **3.** Others would be propelled by controlled nuclear explosions.

____ **4.** One type of spacecraft would take people to Mars in only 250 days!

____ **5.** One scientist's design beams power out to spacecraft using a high-powered laser orbiting Earth.

____ **6.** A few designs have spacecraft sailing on the "solar wind" of tiny particles expelled by the stars.

____ **7.** But astronauts' journeys to other solar systems will still be incredibly long.

____ **8.** Early interstellar travelers will probably be frozen in suspended animation.

____ **9.** Space exploration is one response to human curiosity.

____ **10.** Space pioneers offer humankind new facts about the universe.

Specific Nouns

Specific nouns give the reader a clearer, more detailed picture than general nouns give. Turn to page 74 in *Write Source*.

Write **a more specific noun above each underlined noun in the following sentences.**

1. A guy jogged down a street. (runner; Maple Street)
2. Marta gingerly raised the food to her mouth.
3. Trees provide shade for the entire yard.
4. Jorge gave the boy a toy.
5. Because of her illness, Sophia couldn't go to the store.
6. We will have a vegetable with lunch.
7. Her package came in the mail.
8. He took his vehicle to the service station.
9. A man showered his wife with jewels.
10. Jani rented a video to watch with her friend.
11. Jamal spent the day at a lake and the evening at an amusement park.
12. I have a strong feeling that I will like this girl.
13. The show was reviewed in the paper.
14. Ernesteen was filled with grief over something.
15. A loud noise startled the people.

Extend: Write three general nouns in a column. In the next column, write a more specific noun for each of your original nouns. In the third column, get even more specific.

Review: Nouns

Underline all the nouns in the following paragraphs. Don't forget compound nouns.

Among the deserts of North America, the Sonoran Desert is unique. The Great Basin, the Mojave, the arid plains of Chihuahua—all these are temperate and landlocked. The Sonoran, on the other hand, represents a subtropical ecosystem that flows across parts of America's Southwest, wraps around the Gulf of California, and extends south into Mexico. It covers most of Baja California and half the Mexican state of Sonora.

In summer, the temperatures here soar, sometimes exceeding 110 degrees Fahrenheit. In winter, however, the thermometer's mercury rarely drops below the freezing point. This moderate climate, coupled with relatively generous rains, makes the Sonoran Desert one of the lushest in the world (as far as deserts go). A visit reveals giant cacti, short trees, and a great variety of shrubs. The desert also attracts a diverse group of animals. Birds such as Northern harriers, red-tailed hawks, and ravens grace the skies, while such animals as desert cottontails, cactus mice, and desert mule deer wander below. Both tarantulas and scorpions are also common.

List the following information about nouns from the paragraphs above.

1. The first three proper nouns: ____________________
2. The first four common nouns: ____________________
3. The first collective noun: ____________________
4. The first two nouns in nominative case: ____________________
5. The first three nouns in objective case: ____________________

Pretest: Pronouns

Underline each pronoun below and label it *P* for personal, *R* for relative, *REF* for reflexive, *INV* for intensive, *IN* for indefinite, *INT* for interrogative, *D* for demonstrative.

1. Did you watch the total lunar eclipse that occurred in October of 2004?
2. Who read the article in the morning paper that described what was going to happen to the full moon?
3. Everybody was enthusiastic about seeing the eclipse, but when 10:00 p.m. came, and the temperatures dropped to the teens, nobody wanted to go outside with me.
4. I myself wasn't as eager as I had been earlier, but I wasn't going to reveal that to the others.
5. My two sisters had seemed eager, too; but when the time came, neither looked thrilled.
6. Nevertheless, we pushed ourselves out of the warm house and into the cold to stand beneath nature's dazzling light show.
7. A total lunar eclipse occurs when the sun, the earth, and the moon line up in a row. Did you know that?
8. You don't need a telescope or special eye protection to view a lunar eclipse—the naked eye will do.
9. Some people learn about eclipses by watching the sky. Most learn about them by watching a science teacher line up an orange, an apple, and a grapefruit.
10. These are supposed to represent the moon, the earth, and the sun.
11. But which is passing in front of the other? I always forget.
12. In a lunar eclipse, the earth passes between the sun and the moon so it is the earth's shadow that covers the moon.
13. What gives eclipses their special appeal?

Number & Person of Personal Pronouns

The *number* of a pronoun can be either singular or plural. The *person* of a pronoun shows who is speaking (first person: *I*), who is spoken to (second person: *you*), or who is spoken about (third person: *she, he, it*). Turn to 708.1–708.2 in *Write Source*.

Underline all the personal pronouns in the following sentences. Then label each pronoun. Use *S* for singular and *P* for plural. Use *1, 2,* and *3* for first, second, and third person. Label "you" *S-P* when it can be either singular or plural.

S/1

1. I remember looking down that long, arched, marble corridor and seeing the very famous statue.
2. We—our former foreign exchange student, his friends, and my parents—were spending a day at Paris's famous museum, the Louvre.
3. Fabian said, "Wait until you see the statue of Venus de Milo."
4. "It is the most beautiful statue in the world," he added.
5. When I saw it, I said, "It's too bad her arms are missing."
6. Fabian patiently replied, "Venus de Milo is one of the world's treasures even though her arms are missing."
7. "Study her face," he said.
8. I whispered to my parents, "I am amazed how the stone looks like skin."
9. "Our statues don't compare," Dad said to me.
10. "The French have many statues you haven't seen yet," Mom informed us.
11. Mom said to Fabian and his friends, "You gave us the beautiful Statue of Liberty, and its beauty helps us appreciate these statues."
12. They beamed brightly when they heard her comment.
13. "Your mother loves art," my dad whispered.
14. "I will be glad to see the Statue of Liberty," I said.

Functions of Pronouns

Pronouns function in the same ways that nouns do. Study the chart below and turn to 710.1 in *Write Source.*

Write Source	Function	Symbol	Example
738.1	*subject*	***S***	*You* stopped by on Halloween.
710.1	*predicate nominative*	***PN***	Was that *you* at the door?
710.1	*direct object*	***DO***	Your visit surprised *me.*
716.2	*indirect object*	***IO***	Frankly, you gave *me* a scare.
732	*object of preposition*	***OP***	But it was fun for *me,* too.
710.1	*possessive pronoun*	***POS***	You made *my* parents laugh.

Identify the function of each underlined pronoun. (Use the symbols from the chart.)

This morning my grandmother and I are heading to the north pasture to pick Juneberries. Each year, we make them into jam. Nothing tastes better! I can hardly wait as we approach our gate—and find it hanging open.

A white pickup bumps slowly toward us across the field. "They've probably repaired some fences," Grandma says.

"Howdy, Grandma," yells Trevor as he pulls up beside us. He smooths his dirty blond hair and gives us a grin. "Your fences are mended."

"Thanks," replies Grandma, thankful that no cows escaped. "I appreciate your work. I'm glad you help me." She peers at the fences more closely. "Did you repair the gate?" He nods slightly. "Great," she exclaims. "I believe your mother wants you to paint the porch as well. Next week will you help us move our cattle?"

Trevor shouts, "Glad to," and drives on.

"Let's pick berries, Grandma, before the birds get them," I say.

"I agree," she replies as we close the gate behind us.

Nominative, Possessive, & Objective Cases of Pronouns

The case of a personal pronoun is determined by how that pronoun is used in a sentence—as a subject, an object, or a possessive. Turn to 710.1 in *Write Source.*

Write Source	Function	Symbol	Example
738.1	*subject*	***S***	*You* need to change your clothes.
710.1	*predicate nominative*	***PN***	"This is *she,*" she answered.
710.1	*direct object*	***DO***	The river's current pulled *him* under.
710.1	*indirect object*	***IO***	Frank gave *me* some paperback books.
732	*object of preposition*	***OP***	This isn't about *me.*
710.1	*possessive pronoun*	***POS***	*His* shoes were ruined by the rain.

Underline the personal pronouns in the following sentences. Write the function and the case of each pronoun. Use the symbols from the chart above for the functions. For case, use *N* for nominative, *O* for objective, or *POS* for possessive.

S/N POS

1. I love owning the trunk that my great-grandmother brought from Ireland.
2. What did she bring to America in it?
3. Her favorite flower was columbine.
4. It blooms in our garden, so we often think of her when we see it.
5. She left us a beautiful legacy: her flowers, her trunk, and most important, her stories.
6. Of all our family members, it is I who love the stories the most.
7. They are funny and sad and silly, and I've learned to tell most of them.
8. My grandma also knew the stories, and she coached me.
9. "The stories are yours now," Grandma said to me before she died. "Tell them often."
10. Soon I shall teach my daughters how to tell the stories, and they will someday pass the stories to their children.

Extend: Write sentences using the pronoun *you/your* in the six ways that a pronoun can function. Then label the case of each.

Reflexive & Intensive Pronouns

A reflexive pronoun is formed by adding *-self* or *-selves* to a personal pronoun (*myself, yourselves*). It can act as a subject, a predicate nominative, or an object. When the reflexive pronoun emphasizes a noun or pronoun (he *himself* doesn't believe it), it becomes an intensive pronoun. Turn to 706.1 in *Write Source*.

Underline the reflexive and intensive pronouns below. Label them *R* for reflexive and *I* for intensive.

1. Fabio found himself longing for a motorcycle. R
2. Not even Batman himself could have saved us.
3. The material was difficult, but the test itself was easy.
4. The gerbil gave itself quite a shock from the static electricity.
5. Yes, I have learned that myself!
6. The kids looked at themselves as they walked by the fun-house mirror.
7. We ourselves could not imagine a better concert.
8. You should see yourselves—you're burned to a crisp!
9. Paula has not been herself since the accident.
10. I myself long for a vacation.

Change each pronoun below into a reflexive or intensive pronoun and use it in a sentence.

1. (him) ____________________
2. (her) ____________________
3. (our) ____________________
4. (it) ____________________
5. (them) ____________________

Extend: Identify the function of each reflexive pronoun in the sentences you wrote. Use *DO* for direct object, *IO* for indirect object, *OP* for object of the preposition, and *PN* for predicate nominative.

Relative Pronouns

A relative pronoun *(who, whose, whom, which, that)* relates an adjective clause to the noun or pronoun it modifies. Turn to 706.2 in *Write Source*.

Underline the relative pronoun in each sentence; then circle the noun or pronoun that it modifies. *Tip:* Each sentence contains only one relative pronoun.

1. Farhana, who refused to finish her stewed prunes, told the camp counselor she would rather eat worms.
2. So you're the camper who loves worms.
3. "That w-w-weird animal that I saw," Cindy stammered, "is in your tent."
4. The man who knows too much is here.
5. This blood pudding—which is delicious, actually—is an English delicacy.
6. The Latin Club members, whom I had expected to be boring, were fun.
7. What is the name of the experimental car that we saw?
8. Where are all the people who said they would be here?
9. The main speaker, whoever she was, spoke softly because of laryngitis.
10. Are you the person whose car is parked in the loading zone?

Write a sentence for each relative pronoun below, using the pronoun in an adjective clause.

1. (who) ______________________________
2. (whose) ______________________________
3. (which) ______________________________
4. (that) ______________________________
5. (whom) ______________________________
6. (who) ______________________________

Indefinite, Interrogative, & Demonstrative Pronouns

Indefinite pronouns *(anyone, each, no one)* refer to unnamed or unknown people or things. Interrogative pronouns *(who? whose? what?)* ask questions. Demonstrative pronouns *(that, those, this)* point out people, places, or things without naming them. See page 706 in *Write Source* for more information.

Underline and label each indefinite *(IN)*, interrogative *(INT)*, and demonstrative *(D)* pronoun in the sentences below.

1. Neither (IN) of us has been swimming yet this year.
2. Who left her wet swimsuit here on the floor?
3. No one would admit it was her suit.
4. This is the movie we told you about.
5. Nobody can wait for her.
6. Those are the people from Weehawken.
7. Not surprisingly, many on the boat are unhappy about the bad weather.
8. Who told you to pick me up?
9. Everyone on both teams had to wait for their equipment.
10. Is either of you ready to demonstrate the triple axel?

Use a demonstrative pronoun in your answer to each question below.

1. Which of these did you find in the store?

   ____

2. Where are the sounds coming from?

   ____

3. Which clothes do you need to wash?

   ____

Extend: Write out interview questions using interrogative pronouns. Then answer the questions using demonstrative and indefinite pronouns.

Review: Pronouns

Write short sentences using pronouns as directed. Underline the requested pronoun in each sentence.

1. Use *that* as a relative pronoun. *The essay that you wrote about the eclipse is excellent.*

2. Use a first-person, singular pronoun as a subject. ______

3. Make *him* into a reflexive pronoun and use it in a sentence. ______

4. Use an interrogative pronoun in a sentence. ______

5. Use *who* as a relative pronoun. ______

6. Use a possessive pronoun in a sentence. ______

7. Use a demonstrative pronoun in a sentence. ______

8. Use an indefinite pronoun in a sentence. ______

9. Make *you* into an intensive pronoun and use it in a sentence. ______

10. Use a third-person, plural pronoun as an indirect object. ______

Pretest: Verbs

Underline each verb and write its tense above it: *present, past, future, present perfect, past perfect,* or *future perfect.*

1. Most cartographers call (*present*) the tallest mountain in North America, Mt. McKinley.
2. The mountain was named after William McKinley, who had received a presidential nomination in 1896.
3. Mt. McKinley rises over 20,000 feet above sea level.
4. Early explorers first saw Mt. McKinley from 200 miles away.
5. The massive, towering peak dramatically affects the area's weather.
6. Climbing McKinley is not extremely difficult, but the weather can make such a trek treacherous.
7. More than 90 people have lost their lives climbing the peak.
8. In recent years, the National Park Service has changed the name of the park to Denali.
9. This Athabaskan name means "Great One" or "High One."
10. Many Alaskans hope that by 2010 the mountain's name will have changed to Denali, too.
11. Many Alaskans want to keep the name McKinley.
12. They feel a change dishonors the memory of a former president, and they argue that changing a long-accepted name will confuse people.
13. Because there are strong feelings on both sides, this argument will continue.

List three verbals used in the sentences above.

___

___

Main Verbs & Auxiliary Verbs

Both action verbs and linking verbs can serve as main verbs. Auxiliary verbs "help" the main verb form some of the tenses; they also help the main verb express the mood and voice in a sentence. Turn to 714.2 in *Write Source*.

Underline the main verbs once and any auxiliary verbs twice in the following paragraphs.

In September 1985, about 450 miles off the coast of Newfoundland, scientists discovered the remains of the great ocean liner *Titanic* in 12,000 feet of water. The 73-year search for the *Titanic*, which went down in what is considered the world's greatest sea disaster, has been a challenging one. Because of its discovery, interest in the legendary ship grew stronger and has resulted in movies, museum exhibits, and paintings.

In part, the interest may be due to the *Titanic*'s reputation. When it was first launched in 1912, the British steamer was considered the grandest passenger ship in the world. The *Titanic* measured 882 feet long and 175 feet high, which made it comparable to four city blocks in length and an 11-story building in height. It was proclaimed the most expensive, most luxurious ship ever built. It was said to be "unsinkable."

The latter claim was made because of the ship's special features. The *Titanic* was equipped with a double bottom, and the hull was divided into 16 separate watertight compartments. These added features, it was believed, would make the *Titanic* unsinkable.

Despite its reputation, the mighty *Titanic* did sink—on its maiden voyage. On the night of April 14, the *Titanic* collided with an iceberg in the North Atlantic, damaging several plates and allowing seawater to pour into the ship. The "floating palace" sank in a matter of two and one-half hours.

Linking Verbs

Linking verbs *(be, am, is, are, feel, seem, look)* join subjects to words that rename (predicate nouns) or describe (predicate adjectives) the subjects. Turn to 714.1 in *Write Source* for a list of linking verbs. (Also see page 75 and 714.1 for information about predicate nouns and adjectives.)

Write sentences that use linking verbs to join words that rename or describe each of the following nouns.

1. farming *Farming is hard, but also rewarding.*
2. snowboards ____________________
3. crossword puzzles ____________________
4. puppets ____________________
5. subway trains ____________________
6. rap music ____________________
7. roof ____________________
8. hot dogs ____________________
9. magicians ____________________
10. books ____________________

Extend: Write three examples of sentences with predicate adjectives. Circle the linking verbs in each sentence. Exchange papers with a classmate, and replace the predicate adjectives with your own adjectives.

Gerunds, Infinitives, & Participles

Gerunds, infinitives, and participles are verbals. A verbal is made from a verb, has the power of a verb, but acts as another part of speech. Study the chart below. Turn to 726.1–726.3 in *Write Source.*

	Used As		
Type of Verbal	**Noun**	**Adjective**	**Adverb**
Gerund (ends in *-ing*)	X		
Infinitive (introduced by *to*)	X	X	X
Participle (often ends in *-ing* or *-ed*)		X	

Underline the verbals in each sentence. Write *G* above each gerund, *I* above each infinitive, and *P* above each participle.

1. The Statue of Liberty holds a glowing torch in her uplifted right hand.
2. An American poet wrote these lines about the Statue of Liberty: "Give me your tired, your poor, / Your huddled masses yearning to breathe free . . . "
3. The statue stands on a pedestal, reinforced with steel beams and covered with granite.
4. The pedestal, completed in 1886, was the largest single concrete structure in the world at that time.
5. Running through the interior of the pedestal is a flight of stairs and a passenger elevator.
6. To reach the observation deck, you must climb 192 stairs.
7. Visitors are no longer allowed to climb to the crown or the torch.
8. Representing freedom has not always been an easy job for Liberty.
9. People wishing to visit the monument can take a ferry ride from Battery Park.
10. At the base of the statue, visitors can learn about the history of immigrants on Ellis Island; reading this history is a humbling experience.

Review: Verbs 1

Underline the main, auxiliary, and linking verbs in the following paragraph. Write *L* above linking verbs, *PN* above predicate nouns, and *PA* above predicate adjectives.

People are curious about almost everything. Humans have always asked why. Why does the sun rise? What causes lightning? Today, people have many answers to their questions. But long ago, they lacked data. Instead, they explained things in terms of gods and goddesses. The modern mind probably does not easily understand mythology. Mythology may seem bizarre. But can you imagine a Greek or Roman trying to understand quasars or walking on the moon? To the Greeks and Romans, the moon was Diana's hunting bow and the moonbeams were her arrows.

Underline the gerunds, infinitives, and participles in the following paragraph. Label each one *G* for gerund, *I* for infinitive, or *P* for participle.

Studying myths isn't simply a literary pursuit. Scholars may study myths to learn about a particular social system. Artists, motivated by myths, have used them to inspire their paintings and sculptures. Reading myths provides enjoyment for many people. Discovering the differences and similarities of cultures is another use of myths, especially for sociologists. Myths help anthropologists understand valued customs and ways of life for various groups. Even psychologists study myths to try to understand people. By making mythical characters come alive, storytellers help preserve the ancient myths. Naming space programs and spaceships after mythological characters like Apollo and Titan has helped to maintain interest in myths.

Simple Tense Verbs

A verb's tense indicates when something occurs. There are three simple verb tenses: present, past, and future. Turn to 718.3–718.4 in *Write Source*.

- **Mark Twain *is* one of America's greatest authors.** (present tense)
- **Twain *was raised* on the Mississippi River, the setting of many of his tales.** (past tense)
- **People *will read* his stories for years to come.** (future tense)

Write **a sentence with each of the following verbs, using the tense indicated.**

1. (***read***, simple present) Many high school students read Mark Twain's stories.
2. (***talk***, simple future) ______
3. (***throw***, simple past) ______
4. (***set***, simple present) ______
5. (***jump***, simple future) ______
6. (***write***, simple past) ______
7. (***write***, simple future) ______
8. (***sit***, simple past) ______

Extend: Write several sentences using the three different simple tenses of the following verbs: *see, go, kick,* and *turn.*

Perfect Tense Verbs

The perfect verb tenses describe actions that have a more complex relationship with time than the simple tenses do. For example, these tenses are often used to create a "time sequence" in a sentence. A time sequence means that the verbs in the sentence express more than one "time," as in the first sentence below. Turn to 720.1 in *Write Source*.

Write a sentence using each verb and tense listed below.

1. (**drink,** *present perfect*) Although Mom told my little brother not to, he has drunk all the milk again this morning.

2. (**see,** *past perfect*) ______

3. (**hear,** *future perfect*) ______

4. (**push,** *present perfect*) ______

5. (**teach,** *past perfect*) ______

6. (**hike,** *future perfect*) ______

7. (**drag,** *future perfect*) ______

Active & Passive Voice

In the active voice, the subject performs the action. *(Bill hit the ball.)* In the passive voice, the subject receives the action. *(The ball was hit by Bill.)* Use the active voice as much as possible because it makes your writing more direct and lively. Turn to 722.2 in *Write Source*.

Change the passive voice to active voice in the following sentences.

1. The story about Scrooge and Tiny Tim was written by Charles Dickens.
   Charles Dickens wrote the story about Scrooge and Tiny Tim.
2. Some students will be tutored after school by teachers.
   ______
3. The national anthem was sung by the high school choir.
   ______
4. The delicious dinner was cooked by my friends.
   ______
5. Electrical cars for the future have been designed by car manufacturers.
   ______
6. The Sundance Film Festival is always hosted by Park City, Utah.
   ______
7. Actresses who speak Spanish and English will be required for the play.
   ______
8. A thank-you note will be written after the class field trip.
   ______

Write an original sentence using the active voice, strong nouns, and vivid verbs.

______

______

Direct & Indirect Objects

Direct objects and indirect objects receive the action of a transitive verb in a sentence. Turn to 716.2 in *Write Source* for examples.

Underline and label the direct objects *DO* and indirect objects *IO* in the following sentences.

1. Amusement parks promise people (IO) excitement (DO).
2. Roller coasters attract the biggest crowds at most amusement parks.
3. Each morning, amusement park employees warm up the thrill rides: they take a ride or two themselves.
4. Many amusement parks offer visitors extraordinary rides and big-name entertainment.
5. One clown gives children hugs as another one hands out balloons.
6. Concession stands sell hungry patrons food and drinks.
7. On crowded weekends, long lines test the thrill seekers' patience.
8. Specialty amusement parks offer water lovers wave pools and water slides.
9. The water rides drench passengers and spectators alike, which makes them popular on hot summer days.
10. For great entertainment, spend a day at the amusement park nearest you.
11. The special effects often awe the crowds.
12. How about buying me a plane ticket to Los Angeles?
13. Haven't you earned enough frequent-flyer miles?
14. We could take a trip and visit several amusement parks together!
15. Many amusement parks offer customers special prices after Labor Day.

Extend: What is your favorite activity? Snowboarding? Playing basketball? Writing poetry? Write five sentences describing your favorite activity. Use direct and indirect objects to receive the action of verbs. Don't forget to label them *(DO, IO).*

Irregular Verbs 1

Irregular verbs do not follow the pattern that regular verbs follow when forming the past tense or past participle. Turn to the chart on page 720 in *Write Source*.

Complete the following sentences using the past tense or past participle of the verb given in parentheses.

1. If I had *(know)* known you were getting a ride, I wouldn't have *(come)* come to pick you up.
2. The village inhabitants *(flee)* __________ their homes in anticipation of the volcanic eruption.
3. David had *(ring)* __________ the doorbell four times before giving up.
4. Shelly *(wring)* __________ out the towel that had *(fall)* __________ into the pool.
5. Randall *(burst)* __________ into the room and *(spring)* __________ into action.
6. In her dream, Maria had *(slay)* __________ the dragon just as it was about to attack.
7. I know what a mosquito bite feels like because I have been *(bite)* __________ many times before.
8. Dean *(throw)* __________ the snowball, but after he had *(throw)* __________ it, he regretted it.
9. We *(bring)* __________ a whole watermelon to the picnic when we came.
10. Following the accident, she had *(strive)* __________ to keep her grades up.
11. That horse had not been *(ride)* __________ before I *(ride)* __________ it.
12. The flowerpot that *(hang)* __________ from the porch ceiling was *(blow)* __________ down by the wind last night.

Extend: Write four sentences that contain the past tense of the verbs: *fly, grow, draw,* and *sing.*

Irregular Verbs 2

The past tense and past participle of irregular verbs are usually different words; however, a few have the same form in all three principal parts. Turn to page 720 in *Write Source* or consult a dictionary.

Complete the following sentences using the past tense or past participle of the verb given in parentheses.

1. The sunlight *(shine)* ___shone___ through the sheer drapes.

2. Judd *(sit)* ____________ at the kitchen table as he *(set)* ____________ his paperwork aside.

3. I guess I didn't understand what you *(mean)* ____________ when you said that.

4. When you said he *(break)* ____________ something, I didn't realize it *(is)* ____________ his arm that had been *(break)* ____________ .

5. I have never *(get)* ____________ an "A" before.

6. Her cotton T-shirt *(shrink)* ____________ the first time she washed it.

7. Hakim confronted his manager, and then he *(quit)* ____________ his job.

8. The thief was apprehended outside the store after she had *(steal)* ____________ the CD's.

9. Christopher, who had twisted his ankle, *(cry)* ____________ , and then he *(lie)* ____________ down right where he was.

10. My brother *(teach)* ____________ me something I've never *(forget)* ____________ .

11. "What have you *(do)* ____________ ?" Mom cried.

12. That happened when we *(make)* ____________ your breakfast-in-bed, Mom.

Extend: Write a few sentences containing the past participles of these verbs: *swing, drive, shake,* and *go.*

Review: Verbs 2

Write sentences that contain the elements listed below.

1. *present tense, active voice, direct object* ______

2. *present perfect tense, passive voice, infinitive* ______

3. *past tense, active voice, indirect object, direct object* ______

4. *past perfect tense, active voice, gerund* ______

5. *future tense, linking verb, predicate adjective* ______

6. *future perfect tense using the past participle of* write ______

Answer the following questions.

1. Which helping verbs must be used to create the present perfect tense? ______

2. Which helping verb must be used to create the past perfect tense? ______

3. Which helping verbs must be used to create the future perfect tense? ______

4. List five linking verbs. ______

5. Explain why a writer should usually use active voice instead of passive voice. ______

Pretest: Adjectives & Adverbs

Complete each sentence by underlining the correct choice in each pair below. Label each choice as an adverb, an adjective, or a predicate adjective. (A predicate adjective follows a linking verb such as *be, look, seem,* or *feel.*)

adjective

1. Americans are among the *(heavier, heaviest)* people in the world, and many experts say that our eating habits are atrocious.
2. Too many people concentrate almost *(exclusive, exclusively)* on losing weight rather than on building health.
3. It's a simple fact: eating *(well, good)* promotes *(good, well)* health.
4. We can all feel *(good, well)* about eating *(good, well)*!
5. If you don't feel *(goodly, well)*, perhaps your diet or eating habits are causing the problem.
6. How often do you enjoy a *(late, later)* breakfast or a *(leisure, leisurely)* dinner?
7. It is not only what we eat, but when and how we eat that *(greatly, greater)* affects our health and weight.
8. Just about the *(baddest, worst)* thing you can do is to skip meals altogether.
9. Not eating actually slows down your metabolism and causes your body to work more *(slow, slowly)*—and that, in turn, can cause weight gain.
10. Much like an automobile needs high-quality oil, your body needs high-quality water to operate *(efficient, efficiently)*.
11. Pure, clean water is *(essential, more essential)* for carrying vital nutrients to every cell in your body.
12. It is *(healthier, healthy)* to make fruits, vegetables, and whole grains the center of your diet.
13. If you exercise *(properly, proper)*, you should be *(healthy, healthiest)*.

Types of Adjectives

Adjectives describe or modify nouns or pronouns. A proper adjective *(American, Iroquois)* is capitalized. A possessive noun *(America's, world's)* can act as an adjective. A predicate adjective follows a linking verb and describes the subject (she is *pretty*). Turn to 728.1 in *Write Source.*

Underline the adjectives in the following paragraphs. (Do not underline articles.)

Ontario is the second-largest province in Canada. Although it is the southernmost province, it also extends so far north that some ground is permanently frozen. The province of Ontario is more populous than the other provinces, with more than twelve million people; about a third of Canada's population lives in Ontario.

The Iroquois Indians named Ontario, which may mean *rocks stand high* or *near the water.* The spectacular Niagara Falls lie between Ontario and New York and attract several million visitors each year.

A sixth of the province is covered with rivers, waterfalls, and lakes. Among Ontario's 400,000 lakes are Lake of the Woods, Lake Abitibi, and Lake Nipissing. The world's largest inland island, Manitoulin Island in Lake Huron, is part of Ontario.

Forests cover 466,000 square kilometers (180,000 square miles) of the province. Huge softwood forests—balsam, pine, spruce—are located in the north, while hardwood trees—ash, beech, elm, maple, and walnut—make up the forests in Ontario's southern part.

The southern region is sunny and warm in the summer, so resorts abound. The shores of Lakes Erie, Huron, Ontario, and Superior form its boundary. Low, wooded hills line the shores of Kawartha and Muskoka Lakes near Toronto. Tourists can cruise through the Thousand Islands or take a seaplane flight farther north to hunt bear, geese, moose, and other game.

Effective Adjectives

Rewrite the following sentences, changing the position of two or more adjectives to avoid an awkward string of modifiers. ***Tip:*** **Some sentences are best improved by making the adjectives follow the noun they describe.**

1. I saw a thin, weary, homeless woman slowly lower herself onto a park bench.
   I saw a homeless woman, thin and weary, lower herself onto a park bench.

2. Cheerful, prosperous, smug passersby appeared not to see her at all.

3. The raw, harsh, piercing November wind whipped through the park, sending the brown leaves skittering.

4. The desolate, shivering, half-frozen figure struggled to burrow more deeply into her layers of filthy clothing.

5. Then slowly, with stiff, unsteady, erratic moves, the woman rose from the bench and tottered toward the street.

6. All across the city, other desperate, disheveled, homeless people feel defeated.

Extend: Write three to five sentences about a fortunate person, place, or event. Use effective adjectives arranged in various ways.

Forms of Adjectives

Adjectives have three forms: positive, comparative, and superlative. Turn to 728.2 in *Write Source.*

Write **a sentence about each topic, using an adjective in the form requested.**

1. ***food,*** *superlative* Ravioli and chili are the tastiest foods in the entire world.

2. ***comic books,*** *comparative* ____________________

3. ***movies,*** *superlative* ____________________

4. ***fish,*** *positive* ____________________

5. ***vintage clothes,*** *comparative* ____________________

6. ***video games,*** *comparative* ____________________

7. ***jazz music,*** *positive* ____________________

8. ***camping,*** *superlative* ____________________

9. ***orange,*** *comparative* ____________________

10. ***duct tape,*** *positive* ____________________

Extend: Pick two or three paragraphs from one of your writings. Circle the adjectives and indicate their forms using *P* for positive, *C* for comparative, or *S* for superlative.

Review: Adjectives

Fill in the blanks below with the appropriate comparative or superlative form of the following adjectives.

bad tall generous enjoyable dark legendary cuddly flat

1. It was the darkest night I had ever seen.
2. Sable, a Siamese cat, was ________________ than many cats at the shelter.
3. Some people say that Illinois has the ________________ fields in the country.
4. The cut on his right hand is ________________ than the cut on his forehead.
5. Babe Ruth is, to some, the ________________ baseball player of all time.
6. Today's breezy weather is even ________________ than yesterday's.
7. It seemed that, suddenly, one twin was ________________ than the other.
8. My aunt is not wealthy, but she is the ________________ woman I know.

Describe the following nouns with vivid adjectives. After supplying at least two adjectives in the first column, write down adjectives with the opposite meanings in the second. Do not use the same adjective twice.

1. car	old, dilapidated	new, shiny
2. book		
3. party		
4. idea		

Write a sentence about a subject other than the four above, but use two of the adjectives you listed.

____

____

Adverbs

An adverb modifies a verb, an adjective, or another adverb. See page 730 in *Write Source.*

Underline each adverb in the paragraph below. Above each adverb write its type: time, place, manner, or degree.

time

The rain had been falling forever. Violent gusts of wind swept the streets, rattled the windows, and tried to blow out the flames in lamps. A man struggled courageously against the wind and rain. He slowly found his way through a dark neighborhood in London. Sometimes he stopped and studied a door. Once he went back and forth in front of a door several times, but then he moved on. Muttering to himself continuously, he was obviously looking for something. Finally he stopped abruptly. He no longer spoke. He studied the low, dingy door and now his fist pounded the partially rotten wooden planks. He pounded loudly a second time and a third time. Slowly he turned the knob and the door creaked open. The man struck a match. The walls had been whitewashed. The match light cast very strange shadows. The man hesitated briefly. Then quickly he walked inside.

Write three sentences about what the man sees in the room. Use adverbs that tell time, place, manner, or degree. Underline each adverb and write its type above it.

1. ____

____

2. ____

____

3. ____

____

Conjunctive Adverbs

A conjunctive adverb connects two independent clauses. A semicolon punctuates the first clause, and a comma follows the conjunctive adverb. Turn to 618.2 in *Write Source*.

Underline the conjunctive adverbs in the following sentences. Insert semicolons and commas where necessary.

1. One might have misconstrued his attempt at humor; indeed, many of those present considered his remark distasteful.
2. I realize you didn't plan to spend your money this way however if you want your car fixed, you have to pay for the repairs!
3. "I am your supervisor therefore you will do as I ask," she patiently explained.
4. Will is going to the hockey game in an hour meanwhile he will be upstairs doing homework.
5. Tish likes to cool off by jumping into a clear, blue pool however Ariana is content to dwell in the air-conditioned comfort of her apartment.
6. Now add the flour and mix it in also add the baking powder.
7. If you need me to help you, I will otherwise I want to go to the library.
8. Danni has a previous commitment therefore she will be unable to accompany you this evening.
9. If you can help me with algebra, I'd appreciate it likewise if I can help you with French, please let me know.

Choose two other conjunctive adverbs and use each in a sentence.

____

____

Effective Adverbs

Adverbs modify verbs, adjectives, and other adverbs. Turn to page 730 in *Write Source*.

Add one or more adverbs in each blank to create a smooth, logical progression of sentences. The results should work together as a paragraph.

1. In high school, good grades came ___*fairly easily*___ to my brother.
2. In his freshman year in college, he ________________ discovered he would need to study harder than he ever had ________________ .
3. He struggled ________________ to get out of bed in time to make his early classes.
4. In high school he had ________________ depended on our mother to get him up for classes.
5. In college no one worried ________________ about whether he awoke on time.
6. His high school teachers ________________ had pressured him to complete his assignments.
7. His college teachers ________________ assigned the work and left it at that.
8. My brother ________________ learned a lot that first year in college.
9. He ________________ disciplined himself to take responsibility for things he had ________________ expected someone else to manage.
10. He ________________ attended classes, took notes, wrote term papers, and ________________ made the dean's list.

Extend: Write a paragraph describing how you think your future learning will differ from your high school learning. Exchange the paragraph with a classmate and underline the adverbs in each other's work. Review the results as a team and correct any errors.

Forms of Adverbs

The three forms of an adverb are positive, comparative, and superlative. Turn to 730.2 in *Write Source.*

Write **a sentence for each adverb listed below, using the form indicated in parentheses.**

1. **democratically** *(positive)*

2. **painstakingly** *(comparative)*

3. **well** *(comparative)*

4. **naturally** *(superlative)*

5. **sweetly** *(positive)*

6. **far** *(superlative)*

Extend: Make a list of five to seven positive adverbs and exchange it with a classmate. Write the comparative and superlative forms of each other's adverbs.

Adverbs vs. Alternatives

Sometimes a specific vivid verbs result in stronger writing than a verb combined with an adverb. For instance, *he sprints* is more descriptive (and more concise) than *he runs fast.* Turn to page 730 in *Write Source.*

Underline each verb-and-adverb combination in the following sentences. Improve each sentence by replacing the verb-and-adverb combination with a vivid verb.

1. The death of his wife greatly saddened the husband.

   The death of his wife devastated the husband.

2. Reuben worked hard to maintain the poem's difficult meter.

   ____

3. The river flowed aimlessly through the valley.

   ____

4. The exhausted runner ran slowly to the finish line.

   ____

5. Siobhan drove quickly around the dangerous curve.

   ____

6. The usher politely lead the elderly couple to their seats.

   ____

7. Johnny sat heavily on the couch.

   ____

8. The music played loudly at the party next door.

   ____

9. After our walk in the woods, we looked closely at ourselves for deer ticks.

   ____

Extend: Compare the verbs you chose for this exercise with those of a classmate. How many of the verbs are the same? Discuss the verbs to decide which choice is better and why.

Review: Adverbs

Underline the adverbs in the sentences below. Circle the verb, adjective, or adverb that each modifies.

1. Cast members assembled promptly for the first rehearsal.
2. "All rehearsals will be held here," said the director.
3. Many cast members suddenly got the flu.
4. The rehearsals could have been canceled very easily.
5. The director stubbornly refused to cancel, though he fully expected a poor turnout for the next rehearsal.
6. He was happily surprised to see most of the cast arriving.
7. Cast members read their lines, stopping now and then for a fit of sneezing or coughing.
8. The director highly praised his ailing actors and frequently dispensed tissues and cough drops.
9. The actors certainly discovered what it meant to work for this director.
10. At the end of rehearsal, the director fervently urged the cast to go home and go to bed immediately.
11. They would rehearse again tomorrow.
12. "I will never again schedule a production in February," the director stated vehemently.
13. "This is New York City," the theater manager said. "The weather can be so unpredictable this time of year."
14. The director sighed loudly and said, "I hope all goes smoothly from now on."
15. "This has been entirely too stressful for you," the theater manager said.

Pretest: Prepositions, Conjunctions, & Interjections

Underline the prepositional phrases below. Circle the prepositions and write *OP* above the objects of the prepositions.

1. Though he became ruler of the largest contiguous empire in history, Genghis Khan has a bad reputation.
2. He earned that reputation because his armies not only freely looted towns, but also mercilessly killed anyone in their path.
3. At one time, Genghis Khan's armies controlled most of the territory that is now Russia and China. Amazing!
4. He is remembered for his cruelty and military skill, but he was also an organizational genius.
5. Many feared him, yet people within the conquered territory could travel safely about the land.
6. East met West as scientists, engineers, artists, and other talented, conquered people freely traveled across the vast realm of Genghis Khan.
7. Seven hundred years after his death, historians and scholars are discovering a different side of Genghis Khan.
8. In retrospect, Genghis Khan was either a murderous barbarian or a great ruler —or, was he both?

Fill in the blanks below using examples from the preceding sentences.

Interjections	Coordinating Conjunctions	Correlative Conjunctions	Subordinating Conjunctions
______	______	______	______
______	______	______	______
______	______	______	______

Prepositions & Interjections

A preposition shows a relationship between the noun or pronoun that follows it—its object —and some other word in the sentence. (The nail went *through my shoe.*) An interjection is a word or phrase used to express strong emotion or surprise. Turn to pages 732 and 734 in *Write Source.*

Identify each of the following words as a preposition or an interjection. Then write a sentence using the word.

1. *among* preposition I wandered among all the booths trying to find my brother.

2. *before* ______

3. *hooray* ______

4. *through* ______

5. *wow* ______

6. *away from* ______

7. *help* ______

8. *my goodness* ______

List four to five examples of interjections you hear in everyday speech.

______

Coordinating Conjunctions

Coordinating conjunctions *(and, but, or, nor, for, yet,* and *so)* connect a word to a word, a phrase to a phrase, or a clause to a clause. The elements joined by a coordinating conjunction are equal in importance or are of the same type. Turn to 734.1 in *Write Source.*

Write sentences using each coordinating conjunction to connect a word to a word, a phrase to a phrase, or a clause to a clause.

1. *and* *The senior breakfast will be held Monday morning, and the graduation ceremony will be held Thursday night.*

2. *nor* ______________________________

3. *or* ______________________________

4. *but* ______________________________

5. *for* ______________________________

6. *yet* ______________________________

7. *so* ______________________________

8. *and* ______________________________

What punctuation do you sometimes need before a coordinating conjunction?

____

Extend: Trade answers with a classmate; then correct and discuss each other's sentences.

Correlative Conjunctions

Correlative conjunctions—*either, or; neither, nor; not only, but also; both, and; whether, or; as, so*—are conjunctions that are used in pairs. (I'm *either* visiting Sarah *or* going to the movies.) Turn to 734.2 in *Write Source* for another example.

Underline each pair of correlative conjunctions in the following passage.

Last month, both my cousin and I turned 18, so we decided to donate blood. That may sound strange, but my cousin and I had recently gone to the same doctor, and she told us that we were "universal blood donors." Neither my cousin nor I knew what that meant. The doctor explained that another person could accept our blood, whether or not they had our blood type. We liked that, and the doctor encouraged us to become regular donors as soon as we turned 18 (the legal age for donors).

A week after my eighteenth birthday, I noticed a sign at our local YMCA announcing a Red Cross blood drive. I pointed it out to my cousin, and we decided to show up. Neither he nor I had ever given blood before, and we were nervous—not only because we didn't know exactly what to expect, but also because needles intimidate us. The next week the Red Cross was there, and so were we!

The Red Cross attendants were great. My "phlebotomist" joked with me as he rubbed iodine on my inner elbow and told me he didn't mind needles at all. (Easy for him to say!) He suggested it was best not only to look away as the needle was being inserted, but also to concentrate on something else entirely. Unfortunately, all I could think of was Dracula, but I survived. In fact, we plan to donate again either in two months or in the case of an emergency.

Extend: Write about something you believe in or support. Use three to five pairs of correlative conjunctions in your writing.

Subordinating Conjunctions

Subordinating conjunctions (*after, although, until,* and so on) connect and show the relationship between two clauses that are not equally important. (One clause is dependent, and the other is independent.) See 734.3 in *Write Source* for further details and a list of conjunctions.

Insert an appropriate subordinating conjunction to join the following independent clauses. Change punctuation and capitalization as needed.

1. Although John Riggs lives in Indiana, his mystery novels are set in Wisconsin.
2. Riggs doesn't live in Wisconsin. His fictional Wisconsin town, Oakalla, is realistically depicted.
3. The realistic portrayal of Oakalla is not surprising. Small towns in Indiana are probably much like small towns in Wisconsin.
4. Garth Ryland, Riggs' protagonist, is not a policeman. He has no official standing.
5. Ryland moved to Oakalla and bought the local newspaper. He became friends with Rupert Roberts, the local police chief.
6. The friendship developed. The police chief finally "deputized" Ryland.
7. Both men are concerned about the town's welfare. Their interests coincide.
8. Ryland's character keeps evolving. The novels about him remain interesting.

Write sentences using the listed conjunctions.

1. *whereas* ______________________________
____
2. *so that* ______________________________
____
3. *if* ______________________________
____

Review: Prepositions, Conjunctions, & Interjections

Write sentences following the directions below.

1. Create a prepositional phrase and use it as an adverb in a compound sentence joined with a coordinating conjunction.

Prepositional phrase: *under the porch*

Our dog likes to sleep under the porch, but our cats prefer the chairs on the porch.

2. Choose an interjection (or two) that you have heard and a pair of correlative conjunctions, and put them all in a sentence.

3. Write two short sentences about the same topic. Then combine them using a subordinating conjunction. (You may change the wording if needed.)

4. Write a sentence that contains five to seven prepositional phrases. Here is an example to model: "In the corner of the sofa, there was a cushion, and in the velvet which covered it, there was a hole, and out of the hole peeped a tiny head with a pair of frightened eyes in it"—from *The Secret Garden* by Frances Hodgson Burnett. Before you write your own sentence, underline the prepositional phrases in the model.

Review: Parts of Speech Activities

Identify the following words or phrases as noun *(N)*, verb *(V)*, adjective *(ADJ)*, adverb *(ADV)*, or pronoun *(P)*.

P **1.** themselves
____ **2.** become
____ **3.** tenderly
____ **4.** youngest
____ **5.** had thought
____ **6.** something
____ **7.** intelligent
____ **8.** has taken
____ **9.** Asians
____ **10.** theirs
____ **11.** USA
____ **12.** we
____ **13.** April
____ **14.** intelligence
____ **15.** caught

Using words from the exercise above, write sentences following the directions below.

1. Choose a proper noun and use it as a subject.

____

2. Use the abstract noun as a direct object.

____

3. Use the possessive pronoun in a sentence.

____

4. Use the past tense verb in a sentence with active voice.

____

5. Use the present perfect verb in a sentence.

____

6. Use the pronoun that can be either reflexive or intensive in a sentence.

____

7. Use the superlative adjective in a sentence.

____

Underline the prepositions once and the conjunctions twice.

Queen Elizabeth I of England never married. A single female who was not a nun was unusual, and a single monarch without an heir was unthinkable. Elizabeth used this belief to her advantage by courting royalty from France and Spain, thereby holding both her longtime foes in check without firing a single shot.

Elizabeth also dealt with inflation in a novel way. To reduce court expenses, she not only encouraged the noblemen to give her gifts of jewelry, clothing, and food, but also sought invitations to the noblemen's homes for herself and her complete entourage. Did anyone dare offend by refusing?

Like a queen bee in a hive, Elizabeth was the center of activity at the court. If a courtier or maid of honor wanted to marry, she would have to seek Elizabeth's permission. Sir Walter Raleigh, the "gentleman pirate" famous for placing his cloak over a puddle to keep Elizabeth's feet dry, wanted to wed one of the queen's ladies-in-waiting. Despite Elizabeth's objection to the match, Raleigh married Bessie Throckmorton anyway and was thrown into the Tower of London.

1. Write a sentence using correlative conjunctions. ______________________

____

2. Write a sentence using a subordinating conjunction. ______________________

____

3. Write two sentences using an interjection in each. ______________________

____

____

Sentence Activities

The activities in this section cover three important areas: (1) the basic parts, types, and kinds of sentences as well as agreement issues; (2) methods for writing smooth-reading sentences; and (3) common sentence errors. Most activities include practice in which you review, combine, or analyze different sentences. In addition, the **Extend** activities provide follow-up practice with certain skills.

Pretest: Subjects & Predicates

Underline the simple subjects once and the simple predicates twice in all of the clauses contained in the following sentences.

1. In 1906, Lyda and Helen Conley erected a small shack over their parents' graves, and they lived there, summer and winter, for the next several years.
2. The Conley sisters, who were Wyandotte Indians, were determined to protect the cemetery of their ancestors from destruction.
3. Entrepreneurs wanted the valuable cemetery land.
4. To protect the cemetery, the Conley sisters padlocked the front gate and guarded it throughout the night.
5. You can imagine how this affected the workers who were sent to dismantle the cemetery.
6. At one point in the struggle, the sisters filled in holes that construction workers dug, and they threw the workers' tools out of the cemetery each night.
7. Lyda Conley, who was an attorney, argued their case before the U.S. Supreme Court; she was the first Native American woman to do so.
8. Though her case was dismissed, she gained a great deal of sympathy and admiration.
9. Even after they officially moved out of the cemetery, the Conley sisters made its preservation the cornerstone of their lives.
10. In September of 1971 the Huron Indian Cemetery in Kansas City, Kansas, was officially placed on the National Register of Historic Sites.
11. Lyda and Helen Conley, as well as a third sister who worked behind the scenes, now rest in peace on a breezy hill beside their parents in the Huron Indian Cemetery.

Using Subjects & Predicates 1

Ever since you started studying grammar, you have been told that every sentence has a subject and a predicate. But it's not as simple as that, is it? Because every clause has a subject and predicate, this means that both compound and complex sentences have at least two subjects and two predicates. Turn to 740.1 and page 752 in *Write Source*.

Underline the simple subjects once and the simple predicates twice in all of the clauses contained in the following sentences.

1. Times were hard during World War I, so the Council of National Defense proposed that Christmas be canceled.
2. Their argument was that parents should buy Liberty Bonds instead of toys.
3. A. C. Gilbert, inventor of the "Erector Set," brought presents to the congressional committee's meeting about the proposal, and soon the politicians were on the floor—playing.
4. Gilbert became renowned as "the man who saved Christmas."
5. As a youth, Gilbert pursued sports in the same way that he later pursued business.
6. During the 1890s, he started an athletic club in his father's barn.
7. His only criterion for admittance was that members had to help him with his chores.
8. At Pacific University, he was the quarterback of the football team, and he won more than a hundred trophies and ribbons.
9. He went to Yale's School of Medicine, not to become a doctor, but to become a person who understood as much as possible about the physical body.
10. While at Yale, Gilbert invented a spikeless pole and "vault box" that helped him to launch his 135-pound body to many world records.
11. For many years thereafter, other vaulters used his flexible bamboo pole.

Using Subjects & Predicates 2

Every sentence has a subject and a predicate. Both independent clauses (sentences) and dependent clauses also have subjects and predicates. Some subjects are understood (turn to 740.2.) and some are delayed (turn to 752.2). Both subjects and predicates can be simple or compound. A subject or a predicate with all its modifiers is a complete subject or a complete predicate. Turn to pages 738–740 in *Write Source*.

Write sentences following the directions below.

1. Use your name as the subject; use an action verb as the predicate. Underline the complete subject once and the complete predicate twice.

   Today Manny fixed the computer.

2. Use the pronoun *you* as an understood subject.

3. Use a delayed subject. Underline the simple subject once and the simple predicate twice.

4. Use a compound predicate and a simple subject.

5. Use a compound subject and a simple predicate.

6. Use a pronoun for the subject.

7. Use this adverb clause: *when the hurricane came.* Add a simple subject and a simple predicate. Underline all subjects once and all predicates twice.

8. Use this adjective clause, *which we saw in the shop window*. Add a subject and predicate. Underline the subjects once and the predicates twice.

Review: Subjects & Predicates

Underline the simple subjects once and the simple predicates twice in all of the clauses contained in the following sentences.

1. In 1830, the artist George Catlin left a successful portrait career in Philadelphia.
2. He headed west, despite protests from friends and family, to create a pictorial history of the American Plains Indians.
3. Catlin's wife and son remained in Pennsylvania, and they refused to accompany him to such a "wild and savage place."
4. The artist met General William Clark (of Lewis and Clark fame) in St. Louis, and they traveled together to Prairie du Chien, Wisconsin.
5. Eventually, Catlin went to Fort Union, North Dakota, where he lived alongside the Mandan tribe.
6. After Catlin had gained their trust, they allowed him to paint their ancient customs and celebrations.
7. Warriors escorted Catlin through hazardous country and delivered him safely to his next destination.
8. Seminole Chief Osceola graciously sat for a portrait; it is considered one of the artist's finest pieces of work.
9. By the year 1837, Catlin had painted some 500 canvases.

Write your own definition for *subject.* ____

____

Write your own definition for *predicate.* ____

____

Pretest: Phrases

Identify each underlined phrase as an an adjective *(ADJ)*, an adverb *(ADV)*, a noun *(N)*, a verb *(V)*, or a prepositional phrase *(P)*. Remember that noun phrases may include appositive phrases or gerund phrases and an infinitive phrase may function as a noun, adjective, or adverb phrase.

P **1.** Have you noticed that most of the heroic animal stories involve dogs instead of cats?

___ **2.** Seeing a cat win the glory is unusual, but it's not impossible, as the following true tale will attest.

___ **3.** It was the Rouse family's lucky day when they adopted a cat named Doc from Wayside Waifs, a shelter for unwanted or abandoned pets.

___ **4.** When they had been awakened one night by Doc jumping on them, Sharon and Russell Rouse were at first annoyed with their new pet.

___ **5.** As they sat up and smelled the the first faint whiffs of smoke, Doc scampered away to wake up the three other members of the household on two floors.

___ **6.** Pouncing on the slumberers and mewing loudly, Doc managed to wake up everyone in time for them to escape safely.

___ **7.** Performing better than a smoke alarm, Doc had sniffed danger and had sprung into action.

___ **8.** Through his timely action, Doc was able to save this family's lives and to prevent serious damage to their home.

___ **9.** His work accomplished, Doc curled up on the sofa for a well-deserved snooze.

Verbals

A verbal is a word that is derived from a verb but acts as another part of speech. There are three kinds of verbals. See the chart below.

Type of Verbal	Symbol	Used As		
		Noun (N)	Adjective (ADJ)	Adverb (ADV)
Gerund (ends in *-ing*)	G	X		
Infinitive (introduced by *to*)	I	X	X	X
Participle (ends in *-ing* or *-ed*)	P		X	

A verbal may be used to form a noun, an adjective, or an adverbial phrase. Turn to 752.1–752.3 in *Write Source*.

Underline and identify the verbals. Tell how each is used in the sentence (noun, adjective, or adverbial phrase).

1. P/ADJ Tightly wrapped in their wings, Australian flying foxes resemble miniature Count Draculas.
2. Like some members of the bat family, flying foxes like to eat fruit and bugs.
3. To keep the bats from their crops, fruit farmers have used many methods, resulting in the deaths of millions of bats over the last several decades.
4. To protect both the fruit and the bats has become the new goal.
5. Modern methods include firing noisy rockets, flashing powerful strobe lights, and covering the crops with huge nets.
6. The desire to restore the bat's natural habitat may help eliminate the problem more than any other method.

Compose a sentence using each type of verbal. Underline and label your phrases.

____

____

____

Prepositional & Appositive Noun Phrases

A prepositional phrase consists of a preposition, its object, and any modifiers:

 **I love everything *about the circus.***

An appositive noun phrase renames a noun, using another noun and its modifiers:

> **The ringmaster, *the humorous Mr. Mercury,* gave me a backstage tour.**

Indicate whether each of the following is a prepositional phrase *(P)* or an appositive noun phrase *(A)*.

P **1.** in a bucket

____ **2.** the clown with an extra nose

____ **3.** Mr. Kent's best friend

____ **4.** with a monkey

____ **5.** before flying to Japan

____ **6.** an expert snowboarder

____ **7.** through Times Square on New Year's Eve

____ **8.** the best cook in the world

Use two of the above appositive noun phrases and two of the prepositional phrases in sentences.

1. ____________________

____

2. ____________________

____

3. ____________________

____

4. ____________________

____

Using Phrases Like the Pros

Professional writers enliven their essays by using a phrase when a single word will not do. Turn to 742.1–744 in *Write Source.*

Model your own sentences after the following sentences by experienced authors. Circle the phrases you use.

1. *(one adjective phrase, one appositive noun phrase, and one prepositional phrase)* Laughing and raising their arms, Dad and Mr. Harmel, our neighbor, danced in the falling rain.

____

____

____

____

2. *(one prepositional phrase and one adjective phrase with three objects)* Even our daily news, which for most Americans means television news, is packaged as a kind of show, featuring handsome news readers, exciting music, and dynamic film footage. —Neil Postman, "Future Shlock"

____

____

____

3. *(three prepositional phrases)* Once there was a lot of sound in my mother's house, a lot of coming and going, feasting and talk.
—N. Scott Momaday, "My Kiowa Grandmother"

____

____

____

____

Extend: Write one sentence that includes a participial phrase and an appositive phrase, and another sentence that contains a gerund phrase and an infinitive phrase.

Using Absolute Phrases

An absolute phrase resembles a clause because it has a subject often followed by a participle. The phrase acts as an adjective. Turn to page 744 in *Write Source*.

Underline the absolute phrases in the following sentences.

1. The children, their faces filled with anticipation, waited to visit Santa Claus.
2. Hair pulled tightly in a bun, half-glasses resting on the bridge of her nose, Mrs. Brau looked every bit the stern librarian that she was.
3. Their eyes flashing in our headlights, the raccoons skittered across the road, barely escaping the car's wheels.
4. Wild-eyed and tense, the mustang snorted and pawed, his tail held high—a proud flag of freedom.

Write sentences using the model sentences below. Circle the absolute phrases in the sentences that you write.

1. Jay began to wonder if the computer, its fan humming loudly, was going to crash.

   I hoped my car, its engine grinding noisily, wasn't going to stall.

2. Her hair whipped by the wind, Lola happily enjoyed a grand sunset over the Pacific Ocean.

3. Martinia fumed before calmly walking away from Mr. Henry, her face set in a determined scowl.

4. Its siding ripped from the frame, the house incurred major storm damage.

Review: Phrases

Write sentences following the directions given below.

1. Use a prepositional phrase to modify a verb; underline the phrase.

   We rested under the trees.

2. Use a gerund noun phrase and underline it.

3. Use an appositive noun phrase and underline it.

4. Use an absolute phrase and underline it.

5. Use an infinitive adverbial phrase and underline it.

6. Use an infinitive noun phrase and underline it.

7. Use a adjective phrase and underline it.

Pretest: Clauses

Identify each underlined clause as independent *(I)* or dependent *(D)*. If the clause is dependent, write adjective *(ADJ)*, adverb *(ADV)*, or noun *(N)* to identify the type.

D/ADV

1. When Selena, the popular singer of Tejano music, was tragically killed in 1995, shock waves rolled across the music world.
2. Though she was well-known in life, Selena's fame has grown because of her death, just as with Elvis Presley, Marilyn Monroe, and James Dean.
3. Born Selena Quintanilla on April 16, 1972, in Lake Jackson, Texas, Selena began singing in a band with her siblings at a young age.
4. Selena, whose life has been the subject of countless magazine articles, books, documentaries, a movie, a ballet, and a stage musical, lived only 23 years.
5. Tejano music, which Selena made famous, is a blend of pop, Tex-Mex, and polka rhythms.
6. Most of Selena's fans know that she won a Grammy award and earned a gold album.
7. The critics were amazed that a young woman singing in Spanish with a Texas accent could become a star in both Mexico and the United States.
8. The album *Dreaming of You,* Selena's first English album, was released after she died and immediately raced to the top of the charts.

Review the clauses in this exercise and write your own definition for a clause.

____

____

____

Independent & Dependent Clauses

An independent clause presents a complete thought; therefore, it can stand alone as a sentence. A dependent (or subordinate) clause cannot stand alone as a sentence since it does not present a complete thought. Turn to 744.1 in *Write Source*.

Underline the independent clauses and put parentheses around the dependent clauses in the following sentences.

1. James Lee Burke, (who is a highly successful mystery novelist,) wrote several mainstream novels (before he turned to the mystery genre.)
2. Burke's style, which features beautifully rendered descriptions of Louisiana locales, provides the reader with a lush backdrop for the often graphically depicted violence of his plots.
3. Dave Robicheaux, Burke's fictional investigator, lives and works in a rural Louisiana parish where the history of the South is a constant, living presence.
4. Robicheaux, who is an ex-New Orleans policeman and a recovering alcoholic, qualifies as a highly moral man even though his integrity is constantly challenged by the world.
5. Robicheaux's personal sense of justice often conflicts with his official duty when he deals with certain criminals.
6. Although Burke has created a unique character in Robicheaux, the author still manages to adhere to many standard conventions of the mystery genre.
7. Those conventions, which have developed over many years, are both guides and barriers for testing a writer's skills.
8. Burke's reputation, which already places him among the top writers in the field, improves whenever a new "Robicheaux" appears.

Extend: Create independent clauses (sentences) from the dependent clauses in the first three sentences in this exercise.

Creating Adverb Clauses

An adverb clause modifies a verb, an adjective, or an adverb. Turn to 744.2 in *Write Source.* Adverb clauses aways begin with a subordinating conjunction. Turn to 734.3 for a list of subordinating conjunctions.

Combine each of the first four sentences in the paragraph below with an adverb clause you create from the bulleted sentences underneath the paragraph. Write your new paragraph on the lines provided. (The fifth sentence in the paragraph remains the same.)

A computerized axial tomography (CAT) helps doctors diagnose and treat diseases. A circular scanning machine beams X rays through the patient's body. The machine rotates around the patient. Certain organs can be made to show up clearly. A computer processes the information to produce a cross-sectional image on a video screen.

- **The CAT scan produces images of various parts of the body.**
- **The patient lies on a table that passes through a circular scanning machine.**
- **The machine can obtain many images from different angles.**
- **A patient is injected with an iodine solution.**

Extend: Write three to five sentences about a favorite piece of clothing. Use the following subordinating conjunctions to begin adverb clauses in your sentences: *unless, whereas, as, since.*

Creating Adjective Clauses

Adjective clauses begin with relative pronouns *(that, which, who, whom, whose).* Turn to 706.2, 744.2, and 754.3 in *Write Source.*

Study the two sentences below and answer the questions.

The robin *that built her nest in our porch* has hatched four babies.

The robin, *who made a colorful nest,* used a red ribbon *that she pulled from a wreath.*

1. Copy the first sentence above, leaving the adjective clause out. ______________________________

2. What does the adjective clause in the first sentence add to the sentence?
____

3. Copy the second sentence, leaving out both adjective clauses. ______________________________

4. What do the two adjective clauses in the second sentence add to the sentence?
____
____

Write clauses and sentences following the directions below.

1. Create an adjective clause that describes you. ______________________________

2. Place your adjective clause in a sentence. ______________________________

3. Use a relative pronoun to create an adjective clause about a song.
____

4. Place your adjective clause in a sentence. ______________________________

Review: Phrase or Clause?

Punctuation errors and sentence fragments can be avoided when you know the difference between a clause and a phrase. A clause has both a subject and a predicate and can often stand alone as a sentence. A phrase is a group of words that cannot stand alone as a sentence. Turn to pages 742–744 in *Write Source* for information about types of clauses and phrases.

Identify each group of words below. Use *P* for phrase and *C* for clause.

P 1. through the halls

_____ 2. children slid down slides

_____ 3. to pass the test

_____ 4. making the pie

_____ 5. before noon

_____ 6. singing the song

_____ 7. spring comes

_____ 8. down the street

_____ 9. trees fell

_____ 10. practicing the drumroll

Identify the underlined portions of each of the sentences below. Use *C* for clause and *P* for phrase. In each clause, circle the subject and draw a second line under the predicate.

1. A cartoon is a drawing that tells a story or expresses a message. C
2. People throughout the world enjoy cartoons.
3. Cartoonists use lines while writers use words.
4. Cartoonists who leave out certain details can focus the viewers' attention on a particular item in the cartoon.
5. Children love cartoons.
6. Comic strips are often arranged in a sequence to tell stories.

Use your own words to describe the difference between a phrase and a clause.

____

____

Review: Clauses

Underline the dependent clauses twice in the following sentences. Identify the type: adjective *(ADJ)*, adverb *(ADV)*, or noun *(N)*.

1. I'll explain the assignment if you wish. ADV
2. He knows the person whom he must confront.
3. Josie said she would go with us.
4. That the committee had good intentions seems true.
5. I am aware that you did not keep your word.
6. The classroom where we study psychology is full of artwork.
7. Because the book was a classic, we read it.
8. The teacher who won the award will be honored at the lyceum.
9. The Web site that you recommended has been helpful.
10. We asked the two elderly gentlemen which direction we should go.

Write a definition for a clause. ______________________________

____

Write a sentence containing an adjective clause. ______________________________

____

____

Write a sentence containing an adverb clause. ______________________________

____

Explain why you would choose to use dependent clauses in your writing. ______________________________

____

____

____

Pretest: Sentences

Identify each sentence as declarative *(D)*, interrogative *(IT)*, imperative *(IM)*, exclamatory *(E)*, or conditional *(C)*. Next, identify each sentence as simple *(S)*, compound *(CD)*, complex *(CX)*, or compound-complex *(CD-CX)*. Add end punctuation.

D S **1.** *The Jazz Singer,* the first full-length talking movie, opened at the Warner Theater in New York City on October 6, 1927.

___ ______ **2.** Did you know that before 1927, when technicians were experimenting with adding sound to movies, many people objected to the idea

___ ______ **3.** You must be kidding

___ ______ **4.** If movies no longer showcased the art of pantomime, their future might be endangered

___ ______ **5.** Would the sound detract from great pantomime performances

___ ______ **6.** Silent movies, which required the actors to communicate using exaggerated gestures and facial expressions, could be understood across cultural and language barriers

___ ______ **7.** When *The Jazz Singer* was unveiled, audiences were thrilled, and talk about the superiority of silent movies quickly died

___ ______ **8.** *The Jazz Singer* used a newly developed system called Vitaphone, which combined music and sound on disks and then synchronized the sound with the action in the moving picture

___ ______ **9.** The first "talkie" had just 354 words, but people were flabbergasted and immediately appreciated the new invention that had come into their lives

___ ______ **10.** It's amazing, fantastic, unbelievable

___ ______ **11.** "You ain't seen nothing yet!" exclaimed Al Jolson, the star of *The Jazz Singer,* and he was right

Kinds of Sentences

Sentences can make five basic kinds of statements: *declarative, interrogative, imperative, exclamatory,* and *conditional.* Turn to 746.1 in *Write Source.*

Write sentences following the directions below. Use the subjects and predicates that are listed, but change the verb tense or add helping verbs if necessary.

1. Imperative: *Callie, clean* Callie, please clean the bathroom.
2. Declarative: *spiders, weave* ______
3. Interrogative: *New York City, does* ______
4. Conditional: *people, read* ______
5. Exclamatory: *She, jogs* ______
6. Interrogative: *you, like* ______
7. Conditional: *gorillas, live* ______
8. Declarative: *name of your school, is* ______
9. Imperative: *understood "you," pollute* ______
10. Exclamatory: *ice cream, dripping* ______

Extend: Look carefully at your own writing. Can you find an example of each kind of sentence? If you cannot find a particular example, create one. Add variety and impact to your writing by using different kinds of sentences.

Writing Simple & Compound Sentences

There are four types of sentences. This exercise concentrates on simple and compound sentences. Turn to 748.1 in *Write Source*.

Write sentences following the directions below.

1. Write a simple sentence that has a simple subject and a simple predicate.

Nadia colors the sidewalk with chalk.

2. Write a simple sentence that has a compound subject and a single predicate.

3. Write a simple sentence that contains both a compound subject and predicate.

4. Create a simple sentence that could serve as the topic sentence for a paragraph about a subject that interests you.

5. Write a compound sentence joining two independent clauses with a semicolon. (The clauses must be closely related.)

6. Write a compound sentence joining two independent clauses with a comma and a coordinating conjunction.

Extend: Look in your own writings for examples of simple and compound sentences. Label them. Do you have examples of both? Do you use simple sentences for topic sentences?

Writing Complex & Compound-Complex Sentences

There are four types of sentences. This exercise concentrates on complex and compound-complex sentences. Turn to 748.1 in *Write Source*.

Write sentences following the directions below.

1. Create an adjective clause that begins with a relative pronoun (734.2). *who is a redhead*

2. Write a sentence that contains your adjective clause.

3. Explain why your sentence is an example of a complex sentence.

4. Write two independent clauses that are closely related.

5. Use your independent clauses to make a compound sentence.

6. Look for a place where either an adjective or an adverb clause (768.2) would add an important detail to one of your independent clauses. Rewrite your sentence; include the clause.

7. Explain why the sentence you just wrote is a compound-complex sentence.

Extend: Underline the independent clauses once in the sentence you wrote for #6; underline the dependent clause twice. What type of dependent clause did you add?

Arranging Sentences 1

Study the examples below and the sentence arrangements at 750.1 in *Write Source*.

Write **your own example of each type of sentence arrangement.**

Balanced sentence:
Kenneth Roberts' novels always displayed painstaking historical research and scrupulous attention to authentic detail.

Periodic sentence:
After he had published several unsuccessful mainstream novels, James Lee Burke exploded into best-sellerdom with a series of mystery novels.

Cumulative sentence:
Shoulders squared, head down, legs pumping, the running back bounced off an offensive lineman, angled toward an opening, and exploded into the end zone carrying three defensive linemen on his back.

Loose sentence:
Now rearrange (and eliminate) details in your cumulative sentence above to create a loose sentence, one that expresses the main idea near the beginning.

Extend: Write two to three balanced sentences and then add additional details that change the original sentences into cumulative sentences.

Arranging Sentences 2

Study the examples of sentence arrangement below. For more examples and information turn to 750.1 in *Write Source.*

Write your own example of each type of sentence on the lines provided. For your final sentence, simply rearrange (and eliminate) the details of your cumulative sentence.

Periodic sentence:
Since his work had been mediocre the entire term, Jack's high grade on the final was astonishing.

Balanced sentence:
The author's writing style fascinated readers but annoyed critics.

Cumulative sentence:
Best-selling writer Ernest Hemingway's greatest achievement may well have been his famous style, a clear, seemingly simple style that has had an impact on nearly every modern writer.

Loose sentence:
Now rearrange (and eliminate) details in your cumulative sentence above to create a loose sentence, one that expresses the main idea near the beginning.

Extend: Look for examples of periodic, cumulative, and balanced sentences in your writing. If you don't find any, rewrite several of your sentences.

Review: Sentences

Write sentences that demonstrate the following types and kinds of sentences.

1. (Simple) *My car is old.*

2. (Compound) ______________________

3. (Complex) ______________________

4. (Compound-Complex) ______________________

5. (Declarative) ______________________

6. (Interrogative) ______________________

7. (Imperative) ______________________

8. (Conditional) ______________________

9. (Exclamatory) ______________________

10. (Cumulative) ______________________

11. (Balanced) ______________________

Pretest: Subject-Verb Agreement

Underline the subject for each set of verbs below. Then circle the verb that agrees with the subject. (Do not underline conjunctions joining compound subjects.)

1. More young people than ever before in history *(has, have)* their own credit cards.
2. Credit cards, fairly easy to get with a parent's signature, even if you only have a minimum wage job, *(is, are)* both good and bad.
3. With a credit card in hand, neither a flat wallet nor a zero balance in your checking account *(prevent, prevents)* you from spending.
4. Wants and needs *(are, is)* easy to confuse.
5. Credit cards are convenient to use and great for emergencies, but they, more than cash, *(require, requires)* self-restraint.
6. For example, if Derrick, at 20, *(rack, racks)* up a whopping $3,500 in credit-card debt at 18 percent interest and *(make, makes)* the minimum payment each month, when would the debt be paid?
7. The answer to that question *(is, are)* "Somewhere in Derrick's 60's!"
8. Neither I nor my parents *(want, wants)* that to happen to me.
9. Some young people, of course, only *(use, uses)* credit cards for emergencies, like discovering they have no cash on hand for a new CD.
10. That, my friends, *(does, do)* not constitute a true emergency.
11. The good news *(is, are)* that money-management skills require more common sense and discipline than they do brilliance and an MBA.

Subject-Verb Agreement 1

Whenever a survey of student writing errors is made, errors in subject-verb agreement always rank high. Why? Compound subjects *(cheetahs and pumas)*, indefinite pronouns *(neither, someone)*, and collective nouns *(team, species)* cause some of the problems. Turn to pages 752–754 in *Write Source*.

Underline the subject for each set of verbs below. Then circle the verb that agrees in number with the subject. (Do not underline the conjunctions that join compound subjects.)

1. The graduating seniors *(is, are)* now making important career decisions.

2. Anxiety and confusion *(is, are)* to be expected.

3. Each of the government agencies *(has, have)* published a book about jobs.

4. Occupational outlook books *(is, are)* helpful.

5. Neither Rance nor his friend *(is, are)* going to a four-year college.

6. Many people *(attend, attends)* technical and specialty schools.

7. Both of Rance's parents *(is, are)* supportive of his decision.

8. Neither of Rance's counselors *(was, were)* aware of his decision.

9. Everyone *(was, were)* waiting to hear which school Alex decided to attend.

10. Neither Alex nor his parents *(is, are)* swayed by fancy college brochures.

11. There *(is, are)* a desire among many seniors to get more education.

12. Grades and finances *(affect, affects)* the decisions that students make.

13. Mathematics *(is, are)* the subject that some students have aced.

14. Receiving a fat envelope from the college of your choice *(is, are)* good news.

15. All the forms needed to apply *(is, are)* in a fat envelope.

16. Thin envelopes often *(contains, contain)* only a letter that says, in effect, "Don't come."

Extend: Write three to five sentences containing delayed subjects (subjects coming after the verbs instead of before, 752.2). Exchange papers with a classmate. Check to see that the subjects agree with the verbs.

Subject-Verb Agreement 2

The rule for agreement seems simple: a singular subject requires a singular verb; a plural subject, a plural verb. Applying this rule, however, is sometimes difficult. Errors are likely to occur with compound subjects, delayed subjects, collective nouns, and indefinite pronouns. Turn to pages 752–754 in *Write Source.*

Underline the subject for each set of verbs below; then circle the correct verbs.

One of the best-selling books (is, *are) Tuesdays with Morrie* by Mitch Albom. Many people *(read, reads)* this book because one of their parents *(recommend, recommends)* it. All of us can *(benefit, benefits)* from Morrie's wisdom that *(is, are)* included in the book. For example, Morrie says, "Money *(is, are)* not a substitute for tenderness, and power *(is, are)* not a substitute for tenderness." Morrie, who *(is, are)* dying, *(tell, tells)* his bedside listener and his readers about what he *(has, have)* learned in his life. There *(is, are)* also many pieces of common sense in the book. Morrie says, "Everyone *(is, are)* in such a hurry. People *(hasn't, haven't)* found meaning in their lives, so they're running all the time looking for it." Either the subject of death or the absurdities about living *(makes, make)* this book a good choice. This *(is, are)* one of those books that *(inspires, inspire)* most readers.

Write sentences following the directions given below. Make certain your subjects and verbs agree.

1. Use *thunder and lightning* as the subject. ____________________

____

2. Use the indefinite pronoun *several* as the subject. ____________________

____

3. Use a present-tense verb and the collective noun *crowd* as the subject. ________

____

Review: Subject-Verb Agreement

Underline the subject for each set of verbs below, and circle the correct verb.

1. The faculty *(present, presents)* a freshman orientation every year.
2. Some of the students *(commute, commutes)* to school.
3. The news *(include, includes)* reports about such depressing happenings!
4. One of the classes that *(is, are)* being offered is astronomy.
5. None of the seniors *(realize, realizes)* where they will be next year at this time.
6. All of the seats in the new theater *(is, are)* padded.
7. This is one of the books that *(is, are)* on the recommended reading list.
8. Poor study habits *(cause, causes)* many poor grades.
9. There *(seem, seems)* to be a direct correlation between study habits and grades.
10. Some students *(request, requests)* specific instructors for particular courses.
11. International business is one of the majors that *(is, are)* popular with many people.
12. Statistics *(is, are)* usually required for a degree in international business.
13. Knowing how to use computers *(is, are)* necessary for this major.
14. Do the entrance requirements *(include, includes)* speaking a foreign language?
15. My parents think that college students *(is, are)* more knowledgeable now than in the '70s.
16. Some of the students attending college today *(is, are)* required to attend all classes.
17. Each of the students missing classes *(is, are)* required to give an excuse.
18. Half of the students who *(miss, misses)* class *(is, are)* ill.
19. Most students *(is, are)* healthy, but they *(catches, catch)* colds anyway.

Pretest: Pronoun-Antecedent Agreement

Circle the correct pronoun or pronouns from the two choices in parentheses. Underline the antecedent.

1. A person who wants to be successful must know what *(they, he or she)* wants.
2. One of the things that people like is the sound of *(their, her or his)* own voices.
3. Neither my father nor my older sisters ever pass up an opportunity to tell me what *(they think, he or she thinks)* I should do with my life.
4. Does anybody think *(she or he, they)* will succeed just by putting one foot in front of the other?
5. What good are goals if *(it doesn't, they don't)* take you where you want to go?
6. Each of the girls prepared *(their, her)* own list of priorities.
7. Everyone must set goals for *(their, his or her)* life.
8. Nobody can tell you what *(your, his or her)* priorities should be.
9. Adopt either self-discipline or perseverance, for *(it, they)* will lead you to your dream.
10. A person must learn to manage the distractions in *(their, her or his)* life.
11. Neither television nor trips to the mall have proven *(themselves, itself)* helpful in the grade area.
12. Seriously, my best friend and I are taking a communication course designed to help *(me, us)* improve *(my, our)* relationships.
13. There are fifty teenagers in the class, and *(they dream, he or she dreams)* about becoming communication experts, immediately.
14. The class states *(its, their)* objective is to communicate with many types of personalities.
15. One must know oneself well before *(they, he or she)* can communicate with others.

Pronoun-Antecedent Agreement 1

A pronoun must agree in number, person, and gender with its antecedent. Turn to page 756 in *Write Source.*

Underline any pronoun that does not agree with its antecedent and write the correction above it. Circle the antecedent. If the verb that follows no longer agrees with the pronoun, correct it as well. (Do not circle conjunctions joining compound nouns.)

1. Dorothy wanted to entertain its listeners. (*her*)
2. Carla wanted to go with her friends, so she asked if they could join them.
3. He failed miserably in their leg of the relay race.
4. If you want to understand the reasoning behind my decision, one must review the evidence as I did.
5. His friends asked if he could borrow his car.
6. The car's battery failed on the cold morning because they needed to be recharged.
7. We enjoy summer festivals—it is so much fun!
8. Many competitors invited his or her friends to the chili cook-off.
9. The crowd rose to its feet when he hit the home run.
10. Is either Scott or Kendra taking their dogs to the park? *(Each person has two dogs.)*
11. Each of the girls selected their favorite music.
12. You must learn all the driving rules or one will inevitably get stopped by the highway patrol.
13. One of the trinkets has lost their sheen.
14. Both of the boys are bringing photographs that he took last year.
15. Neither of our dads enjoyed their fishing trip.

Extend: Write three sentences in which the pronouns fail to agree with their antecedents in number, person, or gender. Exchange papers with a classmate and correct each other's errors.

Pronoun-Antecedent Agreement 2

A pronoun must agree in number and person with its antecedent. Turn to page 756 in *Write Source*.

Underline any pronoun that does not agree with its antecedent and write the correction above it. Circle the antecedent. If the verb that follows no longer agrees with the pronoun, correct it as well. (Do not circle conjunctions joining compound subjects.)

1. Terri and Denzel used her heads to win the game. (*their*)
2. If anyone wants to go with me, you have to be ready in five minutes.
3. One of those girls could have lost their earring.
4. Everybody should make sure they have a ticket.
5. Each of the boys is going to submit their essay to the school paper.
6. Neither Fernando nor Robert knows how to wash their own clothes.
7. The lawn is covered with leaves; soon it will have to be removed.
8. Neither the cats nor the dogs travel well in its cages.
9. When you take homework seriously, you will get more out of one's classes.
10. Rebecca and Tina must clean her rooms.
11. One of the cars parked on campus had their antenna ripped off.
12. Your red hair looks great, as do one's freckles.
13. Each of those girls has created their own Web site.
14. Everyone in the writing workshop must describe their most frightening experience.
15. No one enjoys admitting they made an error.
16. Many students are allowed to choose his or her mentors.
17. My friend and I are practicing tact and courtesy because they want to become personal agents for famous sports stars.
18. The amusement park and the zoo are hiring its summertime help now.

Making References Clear

A writer must be careful not to confuse a reader with pronoun references that are unclear (ambiguous). An ambiguous pronoun reference results when it is unclear which word is being referred to by the pronoun.

- **Jerry asked Jack if he needed a raincoat.** (Is Jerry asking Jack if he—Jerry—needs a raincoat? Or is Jerry asking Jack if he—Jack—needs a raincoat?)
- **Jerry asked, "Jack, do I need a raincoat?"** (clear reference)

Circle the ambiguous pronoun in each sentence below. Then rewrite each sentence so that the reader understands its correct meaning.

1. As the space shuttle left the launch site, (it) shook and rattled.

   The space shuttle shook and rattled as it left the launch site. (or)

   As the space shuttle left the launch site, the site shook and rattled.

2. When the bride kissed her new mother-in-law, her hat fell into a puddle.

3. Every time I get my hair cut at the salon, it looks different.

4. Mother took the cover off the sofa so that it could be cleaned.

5. Every time my sister visits Grandma, she comes down with a terrible cold.

6. Lashanda asked her teacher if she could help her.

Review: Pronoun-Antecedent Agreement

Underline the personal pronouns that have an antecedent in the sentences below. Draw an arrow to the appropriate antecedent.

1. The casserole you like is in the oven. Take it out in thirty minutes.
2. The books that Mrs. Fritchie ordered have arrived. Put them in her room.
3. Everybody brought one of his or her favorite books.
4. A college freshman enters a new environment. At first, she or he may feel somewhat lost.
5. Did Jodi remember the uniform? I had laid it on the table for him.

Underline the personal pronouns. Write an appropriate antecedent in each blank.

1. Ricky must meet with one of his advisors.
2. ____________________ wanted their dinner immediately.
3. The ____________________ couldn't find her car.
4. ____________________ read his or her book silently.
5. ____________________ has made its owner happy.

Complete the following requests about pronoun-antecedent agreement.

List five antecedents that require singular personal pronouns. ____________________

____

Write a sentence containing an antecedent that requires a plural personal pronoun.

____

Pretest: Sentence Combining

Combine each of the following sets of sentences by following the directions given in parentheses. Write the new sentences on the blanks that are provided.

1. Most people think they have to go to the country to study nature. There is plenty of plant and animal life in the city, if you keep your eyes open. *(Use a semicolon and a conjunctive adverb.)*

Most people think they have to go to the country to study nature; however, there is plenty of plant and animal life in the city, if you keep your eyes open.

2. In my central-city neighborhood, I've seen raccoons. I've seen opossums. I've seen coyotes. I have even seen deer! *(Use a series.)*

3. These animals have become scavengers. They have become animals that have adapted their diets to include whatever plants, small animals, insects, and garbage they can find or dig up. *(Use an appositive.)*

4. Cities throughout the world have created habitats that provide safe, warm shelter for these animals. The cities also provide generous quantities and varieties of food. *(Use correlative conjunctions.)*

5. Nature abhors a vacuum. Nature starts to create its own ecosystem in any wasteland, riverbank, or abandoned city lot. *(Use a relative pronoun.)*

6. Grasses and mosses are usually the first things that start growing in an abandoned area. These are followed by flowering plants. *(Use a participial phrase.)*

7. Flowering plants attract insects and bees. Insects and bees draw birds and small animals to the area. *(Use a relative pronoun.)*

8. The area is left undisturbed. It will, in time, begin to support larger trees, plants, and animals. *(Use an introductory phrase or clause.)*

9. Succession is the process by which nature works its magic. Succession is a process you can observe firsthand if you are patient enough. *(Use an appositive.)*

10. Urban ecosystems show the amazing tenacity of nature. It is a tenacity that is evident each time you see a flower pushing up through a crack in the sidewalk. *(Use a key word.)*

Sentence Combining 1

Knowing the various ways to combine sentences is a valuable skill for all writers. Skill comes with practice, so work on your sentence-combining skills every chance you get. Turn to the index in *Write Source* to become familiar with how each method can be used to combine sentences.

Combine each of the following groups of sentences, using the method indicated in parentheses.

1. Insects have three pairs of legs, one pair of antennae, and usually one or two pairs of wings. Insects comprise the largest group of arthropods. **(relative pronoun)**

   Insects, which comprise the largest group of arthropods, have three pairs of legs, one pair of antennae, and usually one or two pairs of wings.

2. It has been suggested that one day insects may inherit the earth. This statement seems exaggerated to us humans. **(introductory clause)**

3. The insects' small size, great variety, and fast rate of reproduction have made them nearly indestructible. This prediction may one day be realized. **(semicolon, conjunctive adverb)**

4. Farmers like certain pollinating insects. Farmers despise insects that destroy their crops. **(semicolon)**

5. Insects can be a serious threat to humans. Some insects carry typhus. Other insects carry malaria. And still other insects carry yellow fever. **(relative pronoun, series)**

6. Butterflies and moths have wings covered with tiny overlapping scales. The scales give these insects their color. **(relative pronoun)**

7. The worker honeybee will generally die after stinging someone. The barbed stinger stays in the wound, pulling the poison sack and other organs out of the bee. **(semicolon)**

Choose one set of sentences above and combine them using a different method of sentence-combining than you used in this exercise.

Extend: Look at your own writing. Underline sentences that carry main ideas. Circle sentences that hold subordinate ideas. Combine sentences in your own writing, using the methods learned in this exercise.

Sentence Combining 2

Combining separate ideas into longer, more detailed sentences is one of the most useful writing techniques. Turn to the index in *Write Source* to see examples of each method.

Rewrite the following three paragraphs, making them more effective by combining sentences when possible. Use the methods indicated.

Why do tires go bald? Where does the tread go? A driver puts a lot of miles on a car in a few years. The tires eventually lose their tread. Two specialists estimated that 600,000 metric tons of the tire tread are worn off American vehicles every year! They worked in the chemistry department at the Ford Motor Company. **(introductory clause, participial phrase)**

Why do tires go bald? Where does the tread go? When a driver puts a lot of miles on a car in a few years, the tires eventually lose their tread. Working in the chemistry department at Ford Motor Company, two specialists estimated that 600,000 metric tons of the tire tread are worn off American vehicles every year!

Pollution experts are satisfied that the tread particles are not hazardous. Tire tread is an inert material. It doesn't contribute to acid rain or soil pollution. **(relative pronoun)**

Some independent pollution experts were concerned. Auto manufacturers and the tire industry wondered about the disappearing tread, too. Testing to determine the presence of tire tread on roads revealed that 95 percent of worn tread falls to the ground. The microscopic particles do not stay in the air. The tread that does not fall to the ground disintegrates through oxidation and devulcanization. (It is a chemical reaction that reverses the hardening process for rubber.) Wind, water, and oxygen all contribute to the disintegration process. **(series, semicolon, appositive)**

Write two closely related sentences about the same topic and join them with a semicolon.

Use a pair of correlative conjunctions in a sentence to compare two ideas or things.

Extend: Write five to seven sentences about a pollution concern. Then use correlative conjunctions and/or key words to combine some of your sentences.

Review: Sentence Combining

Using this list of short sentences, follow the instructions below for sentence combining.

- The car sped down the winter highway.
- It careened into a sharp curve.
- It suddenly hit an icy spot.
- The car went out of control.
- It slid into the wrong lane.
- The driver fought for control of the car.
- It slid into the ditch on the opposite side of the highway.

1. Use a series to combine three or more similar ideas.

The car sped down the winter highway, hit an icy spot, and went out of control.

2. Use a relative pronoun to create an adjective clause.

3. Use an introductory phrase or clause for a less important idea.

4. Use a participial phrase at the beginning or end of the sentence.

5. Use a semicolon. (Also use a conjunctive adverb if appropriate.)

6. Repeat a key word or phrase to emphasize an idea.

7. Use a pair of correlative conjunctions to compare or contrast two ideas.

8. Create an appositive to emphasize an idea.

Pretest: Sentence Problems

Correct the sentence errors (sentence fragments, comma splices, run-on sentences) in the selection below by adding or deleting punctuation, capitalization, and words.

African American newspapers that came into existence before the Civil War/ ~~To give~~ *gave* voice to antislavery sentiments. *Freedom's Journal*, published in 1827 by Samuel Cornish and John B. Russwurm. Its goals were to speak up for civil and political rights, promote black pride, and report news about the African American community. This was necessary because there wasn't anybody else doing the job growing numbers of literate, free men and women needed news that reflected their lives and concerns.

The names of some of these early newspapers expressed their social and political mission, newspapers with names such as *Rights of All, Weekly Advocate, Colored American, National Reformer,* and *Mirror of Liberty* sprang up in the years before the Civil War. The slave trade had been officially halted, nevertheless, the institution of slavery was entrenched the numbers of enslaved people were growing with each year tension between North and South was rising. The black presses were both a witness to the injustices of the time and an advocate for change. "No longer shall others speak for us," said the publishers of *Freedom's Journal.* In the pre-Civil War period. In New York City alone, eight black presses were publishing news for black communities.

Of course, the early black presses were not organized solely for altruistic purposes, they needed, as any business does, to be profitable in order to stay alive. But aside from the profitability motive, early black newspapers had a mission: to strengthen, encourage, and unify African Americans. At a time of tremendous oppression.

Award-winning filmmaker Stanley Nelson tells the 175-year-old history of the black press. In a PBS documentary titled *The Black Press: Soldiers Without Swords.* In the film, veteran reporter Vernon Jarrett sums up the reasons why the black community couldn't depend on the white press for news: "We didn't exist in the other papers. We were not born, we didn't get married, we didn't die, we didn't fight in any wars, we never participated in scientific achievement. We were truly invisible unless we committed a crime."

In the 1960s, the black presses began to lose circulation. As the walls of segregation began to crumble. Today, only one daily African American newspaper survives it's the venerable *Chicago Defender.* There are, however, many influential weekly African American newspapers they continue to fulfill the purposes that Samuel Cornish and John B. Russwurm laid out: to report news that is otherwise not reported, to strengthen community ties, and to allow no violations of civil rights to go unreported.

Look for wordiness, deadwood, rambling sentences, and unparallel construction in the unedited final sentence that follows. Put brackets around the words that should be removed. Underline unparallel constructions and write corrections above. Add punctuation and capitalization when necessary.

Today, in large cities across the country of the United States of America, many other ethnic and special-interest communities publish their own newspapers and they do this for exactly the same reasons that Samuel Cornish and John B. Russwurm advocated by doing it themselves: reporting news that otherwise goes unreported, strengthen community ties, and to publish violations of civil rights.

Run-On Sentences

Run-on sentences are two independent clauses joined without adequate punctuation and/or conjunctions. Each could be a sentence. Turn to page 87 in *Write Source*.

Identify each run-on sentence and insert the punctuation (comma, semicolon, period) and/or the conjunction that will correct the sentence. Add capitalization when necessary. Write *RO* on the blank before any run-on sentence.

RO **1.** Since the world began, many animals have come and gone. They have been rendered extinct by changing ecological and human conditions.

____ **2.** Extinction can be considered part of the natural order of things some people question the time and money spent to preserve endangered species.

____ **3.** Congress addressed the value of threatened species in the Endangered Species Act of 1973, and they concluded that these plants and animals are of great worth to this nation.

____ **4.** The Species Act summarizes the convincing arguments of many scientists, conservationists, and others concerned by disappearing wildlife it basically states that people can no longer blame the decline of many wild animals and plants on "natural" processes.

____ **5.** Some species are threatened with extinction because their habitat has been destroyed or altered others decline because of commercial or sport exploitation or pollution.

____ **6.** The uncontrolled development of land and waterways leads to the destruction of wildlife's critical habitats such development must be stopped.

____ **7.** Since the Endangered Species Act was passed, many organizations and citizens have made a cooperative effort to conserve wildlife.

Comma Splices 1

A comma splice results when two independent clauses are connected ("spliced") with only a comma. The comma is not enough: a period, a semicolon, or a conjunction is needed. Turn to page 87 in *Write Source.*

Write *CS* on the blank if the sentence contains a comma splice. If the group of words is a correct sentence, write *C*. Next fix the comma splices by inserting the necessary punctuation and/or conjunctions.

CS **1.** Sunning yourself every day may give you a tan, ^and it also damages your skin.

_____ **2.** Some of the damage, such as burning, may be immediate, but other more serious problems may arise later.

_____ **3.** Premature aging of the skin has been directly linked to overexposure to the sun, people still insist on sunbathing.

_____ **4.** Perhaps the people you see lying on the beaches haven't heard the news yet, but this seems unlikely.

_____ **5.** They like feeling the sun's warmth on their skin, they somehow disregard the warning that so much sun leads to early, unattractive sagging and wrinkling of the skin.

_____ **6.** The sun's rays are most harmful between the hours of 10:00 a.m. and 2:00 p.m., it is wise to stay out of the midday sun.

_____ **7.** It may be hard for young "sun worshipers" to believe that, over the long run, ultraviolet radiation will leave their skin leathery and dry.

_____ **8.** Early aging is serious enough, but the most dreaded effect of persistent sunbathing is the increased potential of developing skin cancer.

Comma Splices 2

A comma splice may usually be fixed by adding a period and a capital letter, a semicolon (and sometimes a conjunctive adverb), or simply a coordinating conjunction. Turn to page 87 in *Write Source.*

Revise the following sentences using the method listed in parentheses.

1. *(semicolon)* Every person is vulnerable to skin cancer, he or she must be very careful about exposure to the full power of the sun.
2. *(period)* People are affected differently by the sun, each person's system produces a different amount of skin pigment called melanin.
3. *(coordinating conjunction)* Overexposure to the sun can hurt anyone, sunblock is important.
4. *(coordinating conjunction)* During the 1800s, most people protected themselves from the sun's rays, it would improve the health of many individuals if this behavior were adopted again.
5. *(semicolon and conjunctive adverb)* You should expose yourself gradually to the sun's rays, you should use a suitable sunscreen product.
6. *(semicolon)* Sunscreen won't work if it is washed off by a dip in the pool, it must be reapplied after swimming.
7. *(coordinating conjunction)* Scientific experts have studied the sunscreen products available over the counter, they have concluded that the products may help to prevent harmful effects of overexposure to the sun's rays.
8. *(period)* There really is no perfect prevention for sun damage, the sunblock products simply extend the time it takes to get burned by the untraviolet rays.

Sentence Fragments 1

A fragment is a group of words, either a phrase or a clause, used incorrectly as a sentence. Remember: A sentence must contain a subject and a predicate and present a complete thought. Turn to page 86 in *Write Source*.

Write ***F*** **before each fragment and** ***S*** **before each sentence. Add end punctuation.**

_F_ **1.** Starting in New England and quickly spreading across the country

___ **2.** America's first amusement parks were built in the 1800s

___ **3.** The first amusement parks started because streetcar companies were charged a high monthly fee for electricity

___ **4.** Wanted the public to ride streetcars on weekends

___ **5.** By building an attraction at the end of the streetcar line

___ **6.** The Fitchburg and Leominster Street Railway Company built Whalom Park in Lunenburg, Massachusetts, in the late 1890s

___ **7.** With a picnic grove, dance hall, rides, and games on a 75-acre site

___ **8.** By 1900, performances of grand opera in Whalom Park's 3,000-seat, open-air summer theater

___ **9.** When silent movies attracted big audiences

___ **10.** Amusement parks all over the country hired silent-movie stars for personal appearances

___ **11.** Originally, American amusement parks were adult recreation areas

___ **12.** Streetcar companies soon sold their huge amusement parks to private operators

Choose a fragment from above and make it into a sentence.

____

____

Sentence Fragments 2

A sentence communicates a complete thought, but a fragment doesn't. A fragment is a group of words that lacks some information. Turn to page 86 in *Write Source*.

Correct each fragment by adding a subject, a verb, or whatever is needed to make a complete thought. Some fragments can be corrected by connecting them to the group of words that follows. Rewrite the following paragraph in the space provided.

Last year during our camping trip to Canada, everything went wrong. Unbelievably, we had forgotten. The rain gear that was packed inside a special emergency pup tent. Which we decided not to bring. The weather which consisted of seven straight days of rain. Our vacation, now a series of miserable experiences that bordered on cruel and unusual punishment. The smell of moldy socks and sneakers filled the once-clear mountain air. Mingled with the smell of wet hair and mildew. Even though we sprayed three times a day with a strong disinfectant. At least it was easy to find our campsite when we returned from one of our short excursions! We thought our week's vacation would never end.

Rambling Sentences

A rambling sentence seems to go on and on in a monotonous fashion (often because of too many *and's*). To correct this error, remove some of the *and's*, fix the punctuation, and reword different parts to create a better sentence. Putting information into an introductory or subordinating clause is also an option.

Correct the rambling sentences below by rewriting each sentence.

1. The burglar fled the crime scene and scrambled down the fire escape and ran down the street and hid under the elevated train tracks.
   Fleeing the crime scene, the burglar scrambled down the fire escape, ran down the street, and hid under the elevated train tracks.

2. Wilbur went to the grocery store and looked for his favorite cereal and found it in aisle three and bought a large box.

3. Natasha went to the restaurant for lunch and ate a sub sandwich and drank a diet cola and then she went back to work.

4. Marion couldn't put the book down because she liked its exciting plot which had many twists and turns and kept her guessing at what would happen next.

5. Audiences loved the book and critics loved it and it was the young author's first book.

6. Lucas was worrying about the interview and his palms were sweating and his heart was pounding and his concern was growing.

Review: Sentence Problems 1

Read the following paragraph and identify each numbered group of words as a complete sentence *(S)*, a sentence fragment *(F)*, a comma splice *(CS)*, a run-on sentence *(RO)*, or a rambling sentence *(RB)*. Rewrite the paragraph on your own paper, making the necessary changes to correct the sentence problems.

1. My neighbor, Mrs. Cape, who is Italian. **2.** Still finds it difficult to understand her husband's English accent. **3.** He was born in Liverpool, England, but came to the United States in 1960. **4.** He's obviously been here quite a long time, however, he still has a strong accent. **5.** Especially when he's mad. **6.** Have you ever heard John Cleese of *Fawlty Towers* fame once he's warmed up then you know how Mr. Cape can sound. **7.** Mrs. Cape isn't much better she starts yelling in lightning-speed Italian when she gets upset. **8.** Things really get hilarious when both of them get excited. **9.** One of them will say something nearly incomprehensible, and the other one quickly responds. **10.** Back and forth they go. **11.** Without really seeming to know what each other is saying half the time. **12.** They each want to get in the last word. **13.** If you were to visit their apartment during one of these "discussions," you'd be sure to go away with a new appreciation of the power of language. **14.** As for Mr. and Mrs. Cape. **15.** Their linguistic differences simply add a healthy dose of diversity to their lives and neither ever complains that language is inadequate and that people need to better understand the communication process before they open their mouths and that listening is an art that needs to be studied and practiced. **16.** No, the Capes' linguistic differences actually seem to enrich their relationship and enliven their life together.

1. F　　**5.** ____　　**9.** ____　　**13.** ____

2. ____　　**6.** ____　　**10.** ____　　**14.** ____

3. ____　　**7.** ____　　**11.** ____　　**15.** ____

4. ____　　**8.** ____　　**12.** ____　　**16.** ____

Misplaced Modifiers

A modifier that is not placed correctly (as close as possible to the word it modifies) can make a sentence's meaning unclear. Turn to page 88 in *Write Source*.

Circle any misplaced modifiers in the following sentences and draw arrows to show their proper place. One sentence does not have a misplaced modifier.

1. The magazine was picked up by someone walking by on the cafeteria table.
2. Running helter-skelter along the shore, the goose on the lake was frightened by a dog.
3. I saw a cooking show about preparing gourmet meals on TV.
4. S'zann accompanied a friend from the animal shelter to adopt a cat.
5. Fred realized the gallon of milk he got was sour at the convenience store.
6. He uses a lotion to prevent itching prescribed by his doctor.
7. In obvious frustration, the students listened as Mr. Herlihy repeated the homework assignment for the third time.
8. Yolanda looked for an attorney to represent her on the Internet.
9. A person can burn 600 calories during an hour of handball at the gym.
10. For homecoming, I got a great dress from a catalog made of white muslin.
11. Rolando cuts a hole and drops a hook, line, and sinker to catch fish in the ice.
12. A diesel engine without special tools cannot be repaired.
13. Scissors for cutting fresh herbs are often the best utensil.

Extend: Now that you see how modifiers can be misplaced, misplace a few of your own! Write three sentences that contain a misplaced modifier, exchange them with a classmate, and correct one another's work.

Dangling Modifiers

Dangling modifiers are modifiers that appear to modify the wrong word or a word that isn't in the sentence. Dangling modifiers are a serious writing problem because they destroy the logic of a writer's statement. Verbals (participles, infinitives, gerunds) are often found in dangling modifiers. If you learn to recognize verbals and the true subjects of statements, you will be able to fix dangling modifiers. Turn to page 88 in *Write Source*.

Correct the dangling modifiers in the following sentences by rewording either the verbal introductory phrase or the main clause.

1. Scanning the horizon, the faint plume of smoke could be spotted.

   Scanning the horizon, we spotted the faint plume of smoke.

2. Afraid to look, the bobcat made Thurgood tremble with fear.

3. Whipping the willow's branches back and forth, we huddled at the screen door to watch the wind.

4. Shaking hands, the bargain was sealed by the grocer and the supplier.

5. After finishing the first three holes of golf, the thunderstorm sent us scurrying to the clubhouse.

6. While crossing the street, a car slid on the ice and almost hit me.

Wordiness & Deadwood

The best writing is honest and natural, sincere and simple. Writers do not need lots of big, clever, or fancy words to achieve the best writing. Turn to pages 78 and 79 in *Write Source*.

Place brackets around unnecessary words or phrases in the following paragraphs.

Growing up—becoming an adult with all the responsibilities of a job, a spouse, children, a house with a lawn that needs mowing and fertilizing and aerating, pets, worries, and debts—isn't easy. Luckily, no one is expected to become mature and wise and self-disciplined and controlled and sane all at once, or all alone. Most young people have an abundance of advice from advisors like parents, grandparents, and older siblings, not to mention aunts, uncles, teachers, pastors—even bus drivers—who are always saying how things should be done, always putting in their two cents' worth. However, the problem with all this guidance is that it is seldom made clear just when or where or how one is supposed to stop seeking advice and guidance and start giving it. Is there an answer?

Some say growing up means letting go of your parents' hands and walking the sometimes scary path of life all by yourself. Using this definition, people are grown up when they are recognized as individuals—with unique, special hopes; original dreams; and particular, personal desires—rather than being recognized only as someone else's child. Still others would say that being grown up means a person assumes complete responsibility for his or her own stupid mistakes, the kind that everyone makes now and then.

Maybe the only certain, sure thing that can be said about growing up is that everyone does it sooner or later (hopefully!), and no two people ever grow up in precisely, exactly the same way.

Unparallel Construction 1

Parallel structure in a sentence is achieved by arranging similar ideas in a similar way. If this is not done, the sentence becomes choppy and unclear. Turn to page 601 in *Write Source.*

Underline the parts of each sentence that are not parallel. Then rewrite the sentence using the instructions listed in parentheses.

1. To become a top mechanic, you must acquire the necessary knowledge, developing the proper skills, and you should get hands-on experience. (Use a series of three phrases. Begin each phrase with a verb and add a direct object.)

   To become a top mechanic, you must acquire the necessary knowledge,

   develop the proper skills, and get hands-on experience.

2. In 1918, he received a severe wound, suffered a leg amputation, and a Purple Heart medal was awarded to him. (Use a series of three phrases. Begin each phrase with a verb and add a direct object.)

3. Inez heard the phone ringing, answered it, and is taking a message. (Use the past tense for all three verbs.)

4. In its energy, its lyrics, and the costumes they wore, the band presented a powerful protest. (Use the possessive pronoun *its* before three nouns.)

5. The car was in the shop for an engine tune-up, a radiator flush, and to have its tires rotated. (Method #1: Use the preposition *for* followed by three parallel objects: *engine tune-up, radiator flush, tire rotation.*)

(Method # 2: Use the infinitive *to have* with three phrases as objects: *its tires rotated, its radiator flushed, its engine tuned up.)*

6. Monique tried out for the basketball team, the soccer team, and she went to tryouts for the volleyball team, too. (Use the preposition *for* followed by three parallel objects.)

7. The once-shy 12-year-old dances with his friends and impressed them with his talent. (Use the same verb tense. Choose either the present tense or the past tense.)

8. Here is where the cold winds blow and the bears hibernate, where a family's income is double the national average, and almost everyone lives in a trailer. (Use three *where* clauses.)

9. I am interested in the stories about Prince Henry, in the way the media reports his activities, and because of the terms they use when they talk about him. (Use three parallel prepositional phrases all modifying *am interested.*)

Unparallel Construction 2

There's a good chance your writing will be more effective if you use parallel constructions. A writer uses parallelism to create rhythm, emphasis, and unity. Turn to page 601 in *Write Source*.

Underline the parallel parts in each sentence below. Next create your own sentence using the same kind of parallelism (repetition).

1. Cicily has begun a strenuous campaign to exercise more, to practice her violin, and to keep a journal.

Our town has voted to replace broken sidewalks, to put in more traffic lights, and to install flower planters.

2. I love our Sunday dinner of fried chicken, mashed potatoes, and creamed peas.

____

____

3. Fans are yelling, music is blasting, but thunder is rumbling in the distance.

____

____

4. Concentrate on hearing all his words and seeing all his gestures.

____

____

5. The program gives women advice for their job search, including successful interviewing, professional behavior, and appropriate dress.

____

____

6. He leveled his gaze at me, pointed a finger, and said, "I know you."

____

____

Unparallel Construction 3

Parallel structures give rhythm and balance, emphasis and effect, as well as unity and organization to writing. Turn to page 601 in *Write Source*.

Read the passage by author Diane Eikhoff from *Revolutionary Heart*, a historical biography about early women's rights advocate Clarina Nichols.

Chapin Howard, her father, operated the town's tannery, a business that turned raw animal skins into leather for sturdy shoes and stout harnesses. An ambitious, public-spirited, likable man, Chapin later owned a hotel, served three terms in the state legislature, helped organize and finance a Baptist seminary in Townshend, and made a fortune with his son Aurelius buying and selling land in territorial Michigan. By the time Clarina Howard was grown, her father was one of the wealthiest men in town, but because he was generous, tactful, and didn't put on airs, Mr. Howard was respected by rich and poor alike.

1. What two structures does the author repeat in the first sentence?

____

2. What type of words are used in the first parallel list in the second sentence?

____

____

3. How are the two parallel lists in sentence two tied together?

____

____

4. How is parallelism created in the final sentence of the paragraph?

____

____

5. How could you make the following dependent clause more parallel? " . . . because he was generous, tactful, and didn't put on airs . . . "

____

____

____

Review: Sentence Problems 2

Edit the following paragraphs for maximum clarity. Put brackets around deadwood or wordiness. Underline misplaced or dangling modifiers once; underline unparallel constructions twice.

A long time ago, even before the invention of airplanes, people used parachutes to jump out of hot-air balloons made for safety reasons. One of the earliest skydivers, Andre Jacques Gamerin, jumped regularly from a hot-air balloon during the early 1800s in the skies over Paris.

The parachute was used in World War I emergencies by the army, having been improved significantly in safety. After World War I, some parachuting enthusiasts formed the United States Parachuting Association, or USPA, which still today governs the sport of skydiving, approving and to adjust the safety rules for the modern skydiver.

Paratroopers, specially trained soldiers widely used for tactical missions during World War II, depended on the parachute for descending into strategic areas. Also known as sky soldiers, paratroopers landed behind enemy lines to blow up bridges, destroying communications, and to cut off supplies and reinforcements.

After World War II, hoping to make parachuting into a recreational sport, parachuters began accuracy and group-formation competitions. In accuracy skydiving, the jumper aims for a target that measures two inches in diameter. In 1975, the group-formation record was set with a 72-person star; but the sport has grown by leaps and bounds, and recently 372 people shattered the record with great skill and dexterity.

Rewrite the paragraphs from the preceding page, correcting the misplaced and dangling modifiers and unparallel constructions and eliminating deadwood and wordiness. Make other appropriate improvements as you see fit.

Pretest: Shifts in Construction

Shifts in construction may occur in four different ways: number (changing from singular to plural or vice versa), tense (mixing present, past, and future tenses), person (mixing first, second, and third persons), or voice (mixing active and passive voice).

Write the correction above the underlined part in each sentence below. The underlined words indicate incorrect shifts in construction.

was

1. Grover Cleveland's motto was "A public office is a public trust," and he is one of the most honest presidents ever to hold office.

2. However, Cleveland's secret surgery was not known until after he dies.

3. Cleveland, the only president to serve two nonconsecutive terms, was only a few months into his second term when a financial crisis hits the country.

4. Shortly thereafter, a personal crisis hit Cleveland when a malignant tumor in his jaw is discovered by his doctors.

5. You must remember that in 1897 a cancer diagnosis was considered somewhat disgraceful and something that one simply did not discuss in public.

6. On June 30, Cleveland secretly boarded a friend's yacht, and his upper jaw and several teeth were removed by a team of brilliant doctors.

7. Cleveland's upper jaw was replaced by a jaw made of vulcanized rubber, which gives him the ability to speak.

8. In August, a story appeared in the *Philadelphia Press* about the operation, but the president's aides denied the story, and the public believes them.

9. Elisha J. Edwards, the reporter who broke the story, was denounced as a sensationalistic liar, but it was vindicated years later.

10. Everyone involved in the surgery kept their mouth shut for 20 years.

11. Keeping the secret was important to "the destiny of the nation," wrote Dr. W. W. Keen, the doctor who finally tells the full story in 1917.

Shifts in Verb Tense 1

Making an inappropriate tense or voice shift in a sentence confuses readers. Turn to 722.2 for information about voice, and to 718.4 for information about verb tenses.

Underline shifts in verb tense or voice in the following sentences. On the blanks write "voice" for shifts in voice and "tense" for shifts in tense. (Correct the second verb phrase in each sentence; assume the first one is correct.)

voice **1.** When you think of famous unsolved mysteries, probably Bigfoot is brought (comes) to your mind.

_______ **2.** The legends of Bigfoot inspire the imagination and have played on the Pacific Northwest tales of a huge ape-man that lives in the woods.

_______ **3.** The Karok Indians told the early European settlers about the huge ape-man that lives in the woods.

_______ **4.** When a Canadian settler spread the story, the term *Sasquatch,* meaning "wild man of the woods," was used by him.

_______ **5.** Jerry Crew, a bulldozer operator, discovered huge footprints near his work site in 1958 and starts a rash of Bigfoot footprint sightings.

_______ **6.** The most famous sighting occurred when Roger Patterson and Bob Gimlin had captured on film a 7-foot-tall apelike creature running through the forest.

_______ **7.** Scientists question the existence of Bigfoot, and much of the existing evidence has been baffling them.

_______ **8.** Bigfoot believers suggest the 8-foot, 500-pound creatures remain undetected because unexplored wilderness has been stayed in and their dead have been buried.

Extend: Reread the eight sample sentences in this exercise. Take note of the shifts in construction that "sound" correct to you. With a partner, discuss why these shifts are incorrect. Understanding construction problems will prevent you from creating them in your own writing, even if they sound correct.

Shifts in Verb Tense 2

When you write, select one tense as your dominant tense. Use it consistently, unless you must refer to a different time, making it necessary to "shift" to another appropriate tense. Turn to 718.4 in *Write Source*.

> **I *like* my job. I *find* it neither as difficult nor as uninteresting as I *feared*.** (The first two verbs are in the present tense, the dominant tense. The verb *feared* is in the past tense because it describes action that occurred before the action of the first two verbs.)

> **He *will go* to Vietnam because he *hopes* to find information about his POW dad.** (When a sentence has a dependent clause and an independent clause, the verbs often express two different times or a sequence of time.)

Underline the dominant-tense verbs in the following sentences. Next, label the verbs that represent a necessary "shift" to another time. Use *P* for present tense, *PT* for past tense, *F* for future tense, *PP* for present perfect, *PTP* for past perfect, and *FP* for future perfect.

1. Tara enjoyed biking. She discovered it was not as difficult as she had expected. (PTP)
2. I expect I shall continue to enjoy my job at Roth's Emporium.
3. In September, seniors smirk and joke about the "little freshies," but they forget that next September they will be "freshies" on some college campus.
4. The twins were born two weeks ago, but they were premature. By now each has gained three ounces.
5. We thought they said the hurricane had already passed their island.

Underline and label the verbs that are used in the following sentences. Indicate the tense sequence using the same symbols that you used above.

1. He has gone to Vietnam because he hopes to find information about his dad.
2. He had gone to Vietnam because he hoped to find information about his dad.
3. When I give the antique collection to you, you will divide it among your sisters.
4. The author who has written a mystery novel will speak to us tonight.

Pronoun Shifts 1

A common sentence problem is shifting from a third-person singular pronoun to a third-person plural pronoun (a shift in number). Also common is shifting from a third-person pronoun to a second-person pronoun (a shift in person). Turn to page 708 in *Write Source*.

Underline the pronouns and their antecedents (either nouns or pronouns) in the following sentences. Write a correction (including the verb when necessary) directly above each pronoun that represents an incorrect shift. (Do not underline the conjunctions that join compound subjects.)

he or she needs

1. If anyone is interested in carpooling next semester, you need to sign up here.
2. An actor may be called back to read again after their first audition for a part.
3. Erin and Anita will be at the presentation to receive her prizes.
4. Before you decide whether to go to college, one should list the pros and cons.
5. Neither Mr. Vedder nor the students were aware that his classroom had been flooded overnight.
6. When such a calamity affects someone, they don't stay calm!
7. The audience clapped its hands wildly for an encore.
8. Both my dad and I like my burgers well-done.
9. For our social studies project, you were graded on overall appearance as well as content.
10. The crowd roared their approval after the fireworks' grand finale.
11. When people witness an accident, your natural inclination is to try to help.
12. Someone left their books on the teacher's desk.
13. Everyone must provide their own transportation to the pool.
14. The flock of seagulls flapped its wings loudly as the dog approached.

Pronoun Shifts 2

Unnecessary pronoun shifts befuddle the meaning of a sentence. Readers expect writers to stay on the same track throughout a single thought. See page 708 in *Write Source*.

- ***They* enjoy reading; but when the sentences become awkward, *you* find reading is a chore, not a joy.** (Third-person *they* shifts to second-person *you*.)
- **Although *children* love picnics, *he* or *she* may need mosquito repellent.** (The plural noun *children* shifts to the singular pronouns *he* or *she*.)

Underline the pronouns and their antecedents (either nouns or pronouns). Write a correction (including the verb when necessary) directly above each pronoun that represents an incorrect shift. *Note:* Correct the second (and/or third) word you underline in each sentence.

1. They enjoy hiking; but when the trail becomes steep, *they* you may find the hiking too difficult.
2. Although the teachers were invited, he or she may be too busy to come.
3. If anyone sees the earring I dropped, will you let me know?
4. If a hockey fan is well behaved, they are probably asleep.
5. When fathers are cheering and clapping, he is probably watching his children play ball.
6. When the employee was hired, they were assigned a parking space.
7. The employees received their bonuses today, so he or she will go out for lunch.
8. Somebody drove into the ditch and then abandoned their car.
9. The rain fell steadily for days, and they flooded many fields.
10. So many people are driven by what his or her friends think.
11. A person who is not their own best friend will be easily influenced by the popular crowd.
12. When the committee met, they voted for new streetlights.

Review: Shifts in Construction

Write the correct pronoun or verb tense in each blank below. (Each verb is in parentheses.) Verbs must agree with subjects, and pronouns must agree with antecedents. Number, tense, person, and voice must remain consistent.

Pilot Amelia Earhart and ___her___ navigator, Fred Noonan, disappeared in 1937 on ________ around-the-world flight. The disappearance *(remain)* ________ one of the biggest unsolved mysteries of the twentieth century.

When ________ was 23, Amelia Earhart *(take)* ________ her first airplane ride and *(become)* ________ hooked. "As soon as ________ left the ground," she later *(say)* ________, "I knew ________ had to fly." ________ was not the best woman pilot of ________ time, but through persistence, ________ *(become)* ________ the best known. And because of ________ disappearance, ________ *(become)* ________ one of the most famous woman pilots in history.

In 1928, Earhart flew across the Atlantic as a passenger in a small plane. It *(is)* ________ primarily a publicity stunt by book publisher George Putnam. Putnam had published Charles Lindbergh's book about crossing the Atlantic, and ________ *(want)* ________ another best seller from a woman flying across the Atlantic. Earhart did write a book about the flight, and ________ later *(marry)* ________ Putnam.

Earhart *(fly)* ________ into aviation record books by setting several speed and altitude records. Then ________ decided to duplicate Lindbergh's feat, and she *(fly)* ________ solo across the Atlantic. ________ took off for Paris on May 20, 1932, the fifth anniversary of Lindbergh's flight. She crossed the Atlantic in just under 15 hours, but fierce north winds and storms *(cause)* ________ her to land in Ireland instead of Paris.

Review: Sentence Activities

Write sentences following the directions below.

1. Write a simple declarative sentence. Underline the simple subject once and the simple predicate twice.

____

____

2. Write a compound sentence. Circle the coordinating conjunction. Underline the simple subjects once and the simple predicates twice.

____

____

3. Write an interrogative sentence that includes a prepositional phrase. Underline the prepositional phrase.

____

____

4. Write a complex sentence using either a subordinating conjunction or a relative pronoun. Circle the subordinating conjunction or relative pronoun. Underline the dependent clause, and above it write whether it is a noun, adjective, or adverb clause.

____

____

5. Write an example of a compound-complex sentence, or write a definition for that type of sentence.

____

____

6. Create an adverb clause and use it in a sentence.

Adverb clause: ______________________________

Sentence: ______________________________

____

7. Create an adjective clause and use it in a sentence.

Adjective clause: ______________________________

Sentence: ______________________________

____

8. Create a verbal phrase and use it in a sentence. Identify the type of verbal.

Verbal phrase: ______________________________

Sentence: ______________________________

____

9. Write a conditional sentence that includes an appositive phrase.

____

____

10. Study the following sentence part by part. Then use it as a model for a similar sentence of your own.

Beginnings are apt to be shadowy, and so it is with the beginnings of that great mother of life, the sea. —Rachel Carson, "The Gray Beginnings"

____

____

Combine the following sentences. Identify the method or methods you use.

1. A cartoon is one drawing or a series of drawings. Cartoons tell a story or express a message.

____

____

2. During the mid-1600s, artists used cartoons to plan a painting. They also planned a tapestry or other work of art this way.

____

____

3. Magazine cartoons are very popular today. These cartoons make people laugh. Magazine cartoons are also called gag cartoons.

____

____

____

Write the correct pronoun in each blank below.

1. Neither Stephanie nor Sharmin will be at the ceremony to receive her award.

2. Last year, Bill made a nice acceptance speech when the school gave ________ its highest award.

3. If you have any books by Norman Mailer, please loan ________ to me.

4. The party committee gave ________ endorsement to an unexpected candidate.

5. Both Juan and Adriana plan to pick up ________ sports equipment.

6. Matilda sent a note to thank ________ aunt for the gift.

Circle the verb in parentheses that agrees with its subject.

1. Geraldo *(is, are)* taking some time away from his job.

2. He and his wife always *(visit, visits)* the place she *(have, has)* chosen.

3. Gini *(want, wants)* to bring Pete, their dog, with them this year.

4. Neither of them *(think, thinks)* Pete should be left in the car overnight.

5. Geraldo or Gini *(need, needs)* to find a hotel that accepts pets.

6. All of the hotels that accept pets *(require, requires)* a pet deposit.

7. One of the hotels *(accept, accepts)* only pets weighing less than 15 pounds.

8. All hotel staff members *(has, have)* the authority to enforce this rule.

Choose the entry from column B that best describes the problem in each sentence in column A. Write the corresponding letter on the blank.

Column A

__g__ **1.** Scratching his long, white beard, the five-year-old boy ran to talk to Santa.

_____ **2.** The burglar fled the scene and ran down the fire escape and jumped onto the street and hid under the elevated train tracks.

_____ **3.** Planning a career is not an easy task, it should begin as early in your high school years as possible.

_____ **4.** People shouldn't spread germs at work when you're sick.

_____ **5.** The child, recognized as an individual.

_____ **6.** Finishing the business section of the paper, the train pulled into the station right on time.

_____ **7.** Keep all your options open welcome new experiences.

_____ **8.** Who knows when the last remaining, final piece of the puzzle may appear or reveal itself?

_____ **9.** Ravi knows how to play the guitar, the piano, and he toots on the clarinet.

Column B

a. Fragment

b. Comma splice

c. Run-on sentence

d. Wordiness

e. Unparallel structure

f. Dangling modifier

g. Misplaced modifier

h. Rambling sentence

i. Shift in construction